TABLE OF CONTENTS

INTRODUCTION

Organization of the Teacher's Manual

This Teacher's Manual for the second edition of *New Directions: Reading, Writing, and Critical Thinking* includes an introductory section followed by suggestions and comments on specific readings and activities of the Student's Book. The introduction gives an overview of the book's aims and structure, a review of the book's pedagogical approaches, and ideas about how to use the readings and activities in the text. The chapter comments and suggestions include a discussion of the topic and writing technique in each chapter, a summary of the content of the readings, typical student responses to selections, teaching tips, and sample answers to questions.

Not all of the exercises found in the Student's Book are covered in the Teacher's Manual. Answers and comments have been included only for activities that are thought to be most useful for teachers.

Overview of the Text

New Directions is a thematically organized reading/writing text for ESL, EFL, and native English-speaking students who are studying, or preparing for study, at a college or a university where English is the medium of instruction. Designed to help students meet the demands of reading and writing assignments in postsecondary content classes, the book provides challenging activities that promote the higher-order thinking abilities of analysis, synthesis, interpretation, evaluation, and application. Stressing the acquisition of skills necessary for academic success, *New Directions* provides strategies and exercises that help develop students' ability to think and read critically and to write effectively in narrative, expository, and argumentative modes. Diverse, authentic readings are included in each chapter, as well as opportunities for formal and informal writing, such as summaries, essays, reports, and personal journal entries. Considerable practice is also provided with the development of academic vocabulary in realistic and personalized contexts.

The five chapters center on themes that are relevant to students' personal, academic, and professional lives. Each chapter introduces a writing technique: main ideas and supporting details, purpose and audience, figures of speech, summarizing and paraphrasing, and tone. Students first observe the ways in which the authors of the readings use the technique, and then they practice it themselves in short writing assignments. Between the second and third chapters of the book is a reference guide, *The Essentials of Writing*, which helps students structure an essay, work through the writing process, and incorporate sources.

New
Second Edition
DIRECTIONS

Reading, Writing, and Critical Thinking

TEACHER'S MANUAL

PETER S. GARDNER

CAMBRIDGE
UNIVERSITY PRESS

CAMBRIDGE UNIVERSITY PRESS
Cambridge, New York, Melbourne, Madrid, Cape Town,
Singapore, São Paulo, Delhi, Mexico City

Cambridge University Press
32 Avenue of the Americas, New York, NY 10013–2473, USA

www.cambridge.org
Information on this title: www.cambridge.org/9780521541732

First published 2005
5th printing 2012

Printed in the United States of America

A catalog record for this book is available from the British Library.

ISBN 978-0-521-54172-5 student's book
ISBN 978-0-521-54173-2 teacher's book

Book design and layout services: Page Designs International

Pedagogy

New Directions stresses a content-based approach to the development of reading, writing, and critical thinking abilities. This integrated-skills orientation promotes language development in interrelated and realistic contexts. By emphasizing the expression, interpretation, and negotiation of meaning rather than the practice of discrete reading and writing skills, this whole-language approach fosters the linguistic and thinking abilities that students will need in order to succeed in their college and university classes. The diverse reading, writing, note-taking, and discussion activities, as well as visual materials such as photographs, charts, graphs, and tables, actively engage students in the text. Students grapple with important social issues, encounter multiple sources and perspectives, synthesize information, and reflect critically on the views expressed by the authors and their classmates. The book stresses a process approach to writing, where students plan, draft, and revise their essays; think about issues of content, purpose, and audience; and develop their own voices as writers. Many of the pre- and postreading activities in the book are collaborative, with students sharing personal opinions and experiences and working together to answer questions and complete tasks in and out of class.

Using the Text

New Directions contains more readings and exercises than most teachers would use in a single semester. Teachers shouldn't feel that they need to "get through the book" from cover to cover. A variety of reading, writing, and critical thinking activities appear in the text, and teachers are encouraged to select the ones they think will be most interesting to their students and to add others. The Core Readings in the text are longer and contain extensive exercise material. The Additional Readings are usually shorter and are surrounded by fewer exercises. They are intended to give students practice in reading different genres including fiction and poetry. Throughout the Teacher's Manual, supplementary readings and activities dealing with the chapter topics are recommended. When Web sites are mentioned in the Student's Book, the titles are included in the Teacher's Manual in the event that the URL has changed. This way, students can search for the title of the Web site and still complete the activity.

The chapters in *New Directions* can be read in any order. Teachers may select the chapters based on the writing technique emphasized in each or on the themes that most interest the students. Instructors working with students from a variety of cultural backgrounds may wish to start with the first chapter, which focuses on intercultural communication and presents a framework for understanding cultural differences. This chapter also provides practice with the most basic of the reading/writing strategies introduced in the book: identifying main ideas and supporting details.

The Essentials of Writing

The Essentials of Writing, offset in colored pages, helps students learn about the structure of a piece of academic writing, the stages of the writing process, and the use of sources. Since the way an author writes depends on the subject, audience, and purpose, these materials provide strategies for writing rather than prescriptions. Students are continually reminded that good writing is a process rather than simply a product. They are encouraged to take their time and to experiment as they discover ideas, develop and organize them, and revise material to achieve the best effect.

Teachers might use this writing guide in two ways. First, the reference materials can be related to the chapter readings as the class looks at the ways in which writers organize, develop, and document their ideas. Second, students can practice the writing strategies themselves as part of their assignments. Checklists and diagrams are provided throughout the writing guide to help students with various aspects of the writing process.

CHAPTER ONE

Intercultural Communication

The theme of this chapter is cross-cultural similarities and differences in values, beliefs, and practices and the conflicts and misunderstandings that arise when people from different cultures interact. The readings and activities explore such issues as verbal and nonverbal communication, perceptions of time, cultural adjustment, and concepts of friendship.

The writing technique in the chapter involves identifying main ideas and supporting details. In addition to working with students on this skill within the context of chapter readings, instructors should concentrate on students' own writing – the need to express their main points clearly, to back them up with specific details, and to balance generalizations and concrete evidence.

CORE READING 1 (pages 5–13)
American Values and Assumptions   Gary Althen

In this chapter excerpt, Althen focuses on nine central values and assumptions shared by the majority of people living in the United States. He contrasts these cultural patterns with those of other nations and describes the types of problems and misunderstandings that can occur when people from different cultures, with diverse beliefs and perceptions, interact.

When discussing this reading, it is important to remind students that the United States is a multicultural society (see the chart on page 94 in the Student's Book), with a variety of value orientations and that the patterns Althen identifies will not apply to every cultural group. However, because these groups live within the dominant culture, they often share many of the mainstream values that Althen considers.

Agreeing and Disagreeing   (page 4)

Teachers might return to this activity after students have read the selection and ask them to identify the values reflected in each of the ten statements.

Main Ideas (pages 13–14)

1 "The most important thing to understand about Americans is probably their devotion to individualism" (par. 3). The fundamental value of a "free, self-reliant individual" (par. 14) is closely related to all the other cultural values Althen discusses and helps explain many aspects of U.S. behavior and thinking: child rearing (pars. 4–9, 14), independence and personal freedom (pars. 10–12), heroism (par. 14), common idiomatic expressions (par. 14), competition (par. 15), privacy (pars. 16–17), and communication style (pars. 40–47).

2 Althen focuses on two major consequences of cultural variations in values and assumptions: first, negative value judgments, which often result in intercultural misunderstandings (pars. 10, 11, 28, 32, 37) and second, difficulties people from different cultures have understanding each other and the negative feelings caused by these differences (pars. 16, 17, 20, 21, 29).

3 In the chapter "American Values and Assumptions," Gary Althen contends that cultural variations exist in values and assumptions relating to human nature, social relationships, activity, time, and people's relation to nature. He maintains that this can cause problems when individuals from different parts of the world interact. (See the negative value judgments and misunderstandings mentioned in Question 2, above.)

Although this is the underlying idea of the excerpt, students often provide another possible answer to this question: Althen's main point is to introduce visitors to the United States to the predominant cultural values and assumptions of the country, especially individualism, in order to minimize intercultural tension and misunderstanding.

Reflecting on Content (page 14)

1 Examples of cultural values that overlap with and support each other are individualism and competition; individualism and privacy; individualism and equality; individualism and achievement; individualism and directness; equality and informality; informality and directness; time and the future; and time and progress.

2 Students often focus on cultural differences in the following values: individualism versus group orientation as seen in child rearing, competition, and privacy; equality versus authoritarianism as seen in social relationships and institutions; informality versus formality illustrated in speech, dress, and social relationships; a future versus a past time orientation played out in tradition, daily schedules, and action; and direct versus indirect communication styles often seen in conflict management, public displays of emotion, and saying yes or no.

3 This question presents a good opportunity to review the distinction between "objective" and "subjective." Usually students feel that Althen is objective

in his writing and that it is difficult to get a sense of how he feels about the issues he raises. This sense of objectivity is enhanced by Althen's qualification of statements in paragraphs 18 and 44 and his inclusion of negative value judgments made by Americans about people of other cultures and vice versa. (See Question 2 in *Main Ideas*.) Sometimes, however, students feel that Althen is glorifying U.S. culture, especially the value of individualism. This sense comes perhaps more from a lengthy discussion of the value rather than from any positive value judgments that Althen actually makes.

A Writer's Technique: *Supporting Details* (pages 14–15)

This activity provides an opportunity to stress the importance of supporting details in writing. Writers use details such as examples, facts, statistics, reasons, anecdotes, quotations, and definitions to back up their generalizations. Since student writing often shows weaknesses in the development of ideas through supporting detail, teachers should plan to spend sufficient time on this activity and the corresponding exercises on pages 23, 24, and 32.

1 The values of independence and self-reliance are very strong in the United States.

2 Americans value privacy in their daily lives.

3 Americans think that nature should be controlled and used in the service of human beings.

4 The American stress on doing things efficiently reflects a future time orientation.

5 The value placed on action is fundamental to life in the United States.

Vocabulary: *Negative Prefixes* (pages 15–16)

Although there are various guidelines regarding the correct use of negative prefixes, teachers might mention that the most common ones are *un-* and *in-* (*unbelievable, incredible*). *In-/im-/il-/ir-* are phonologically determined by the consonant that follows them. *Im-* is used if the following consonant is *b, p,* or *m* (*imbalance, improper, immature*). Use *il-* if the stem begins with *l* (*illegal, illegitimate*) and *ir-* if the stem begins with *r* (*irregular, irrational*).

1 a. undesirable b. disbelief c. unspecified d. immature e. indecisive
f. disrespectful g. informal h. impatient i. non-European (un-European is also possible) j. inhuman (the variation *unhuman* appears in the text) k. inadequately l. unemotional (nonemotional is also possible)

2 a. abnormal b. disassociated, unassociated c. unappealing d. irreverence e. inconsiderate f. untypical, nontypical g. improper h. disinclined i. illogical j. misbehave

Discussion (pages 16–17)

1 While discussing values and assumptions, students often refer to cultural differences in attitudes and behaviors relating to individualism versus collectivism, formality versus informality, past versus future time orientation, and direct versus indirect communication style. Topics that often come up include differences in educational and child-rearing practices, interpersonal relationships, use of mass media, and daily activities.

2 Students often enjoy discussing English proverbs and the equivalents in other languages. When discussing the cultural values that the proverbs reflect, students should refer to the nine values that Althen discusses but also feel free to add ones that he doesn't mention. Following are some of the values reflected in the proverbs.

   a. practicality, action, future
   b. individualism, self-reliance, self-improvement, initiative
   c. individualism and independence
   d. realism, practicality, individualism, equality
   e. assertiveness, directness, action
   f. thriftiness and future
   g. patience and pragmatism
   h. time, action, work ethic
   i. privacy, private property, patriarchy
   j. efficiency, practicality, realism

3 In order to help students locate relevant interviews, instructors might introduce the term *oral history* (the recording of people's experiences and recollections) and suggest that students research the term using the library and/or Internet. For several collections of oral histories, see the comments under *Discussion*, Question 2, on page 64 of this manual. A Web search for "intercultural interview" and "intercultural oral history" may also yield useful results.

CORE READING 2 (pages 19–22)
Where Do We Stand? Lisa Davis

In this short article, Davis focuses on cross-cultural differences in the use of personal space and on the conflicts and misunderstandings that often arise from these differences. She maintains that, with enough training or coaching, people can learn the nonverbal habits of other cultures and minimize intercultural problems.

Students usually find the subject of nonverbal communication very interesting and actively participate in the pre- and post-reading activities. They especially enjoy sharing gestures and other forms of nonverbal behavior from various cultures and discussing cross-cultural differences and misunderstandings.

Journal Writing (page 18)

After students write in their journals, instructors might brainstorm different forms of nonverbal communication with them: *kinesics* (body movements); *proxemics* (use of personal and social space); *haptics* (touching); *paralanguage* (volume, pitch, rhythm, tone, etc.); *olfactics* (sense of smell); *chronemics* (a culture's orientation to time); *silence* (such as in conversational turn-taking); and *appearance*.

Previewing the Topic (page 18)

Albert Mehrabian, a social psychologist and author of the book *Nonverbal Communication* (Chicago: Aldine-Atherton, 1972), maintains that the overall emotional impact of a message is composed of a 7 percent verbal element, a 38 percent vocal element, and a 55 percent nonverbal (primarily facial) element. Of course, the percentages are relative and depend on the type of verbal interaction, but Mehrabian's point is that a large component of interpersonal communication is conveyed through nonverbal channels.

Main Ideas (page 23)

1 Types of nonverbal communication mentioned in the reading include the following: personal space (par. 2), eye contact (pars. 3, 6, 7, 11), touching (pars. 7, 14, 17), greetings (hand shaking: pars. 6, 15; kissing: par. 15; bowing: par. 15), smiling (pars. 7, 8, 12), body orientation and posture (pars. 3, 8), and smell (pars. 5, 14). This list can be grouped under proxemics, haptics, and olfactics as mentioned in *Journal Writing* above.

2 The major cause of the nonverbal conflicts is the tendency for people to interpret the nonverbal patterns of another culture in terms of the patterns within their own culture. This ethnocentric viewing of reality often results in misinterpretations (par. 4), negative value judgments (pars. 8, 10–12), and feelings of discomfort (pars. 1–2, 6–7, 9, 12).

3 In her article "Where Do We Stand?" Lisa Davis maintains that cultural differences exist in the use of personal space, and this often leads to intercultural conflicts and misunderstandings, especially in an increasingly global world. With enough training and practice, however, people can learn the nonverbal patterns of other cultures and minimize problems.

Reflecting on Content (page 23)

1 Both verbal and nonverbal languages are "a subtle code, but one we use and interpret easily, indeed automatically, having absorbed the vocabulary from infancy" (par. 3). Both have a universal cultural and personal component, a grammar and vocabulary, and various social functions. Both vary "from culture to culture, from group to group within a single country, even between

the sexes" and have "distinctive accents, confusing umlauts" (par. 4). Both are subject to "misinterpretation" (par. 4). Both involve a system of signs and symbols that are ordered in certain ways, that can be understood by a group of people, and that are used to communicate ideas and feelings. Both, when learned, can help facilitate adjustment to a new culture.

2 Global differences in nonverbal communication are the result of geographical, social, and cultural factors, including variations in values, perceptions, beliefs, and behaviors. There are very few contexts in which nonverbal behaviors are the same around the world; that is, although all forms of nonverbal behavior are seen in all cultures, the social contexts in which the behaviors are displayed vary from culture to culture. Specialists believe that the only form of nonverbal communication that is universal and not learned is facial expressions reflecting basic human emotions: happiness, sadness, anger, fear, surprise, and disgust. (See *Discussion* Question 2 on the following page.) Yet the rules governing the nonverbal expression of these emotions vary cross-culturally.

3 In paragraph 17, Davis says, "Luckily, given coaching and time, it seems easier to acculturate to foreign habits of contact." Throughout the article, she mentions different training programs that can help people become acquainted with the nonverbal patterns of various cultures and avoid misunderstandings (pars. 4–5, 8, 16–17). If people become more aware of the nonverbal behavior of other cultures, they will be less likely to make negative value judgments that often lead to conflict. (For examples of such value judgments, see pars. 8, 10–12.)

A Writer's Technique: *Supporting Details*   (pages 23–24)

1 Americans use more direct eye contact than do Japanese (par. 6); South Americans converse at a closer distance and establish more direct eye contact than do Northern Europeans (par. 7); Saudi Arabian men often hold hands while walking down the street together, and American men don't (par. 17).

2 Men tend to converse at a greater distance than do women (pars. 8–9), and women establish more eye contact than do men (par. 9).

3 Russians are a high-contact people, whereas Estonians are a noncontact group (par. 10). Caucasian schoolteachers associate a student's avoidance of eye contact with deception, whereas Asian students see such avoidance as a sign of respect (par. 11).

4 Caucasian schoolteachers view a student's avoidance of eye contact as a sign of deception, whereas Asian students see such avoidance as a sign of respect (par. 11). An American who is used to standing in the corner of an elevator and avoiding eye contact with other people will feel that something is wrong if someone stands only a few inches away (par. 12). The American mentioned in paragraph 1 feels "vaguely bullied" (par. 2) and the Arab "unaccountably chilled" (par. 2).

Vocabulary: *Idioms*   (page 24)

There are a large number of idioms in English based on parts of the body. Here is a brief list: *to pull someone's leg; to turn your nose up at something; to give someone the cold shoulder; to bang your head against the wall; to have cold feet; to have your lips sealed;* and *to be on the tip of your tongue.*

Discussion   (pages 25–26)

1 In this activity, students nonverbally illustrate a number of comments, situations, and emotions. The emotions happiness, sadness, anger, fear, surprise, and disgust are the same as those reflected in six of the seven facial expressions in the next activity.

2 a. happy b. surprised c. disgusted d. contemptuous (or skeptical) e. sad
   f. afraid g. angry

   Social psychologist Paul Ekman showed pictures *a–c* and *e–f* to numerous Western and non-Western cultures and found great consensus in the labeling of emotions. His studies also show that the facial expression for contempt/skepticism (letter d) is also likely universal.

3 For a list of print and online resources dealing with nonverbal communication, see "ComResources Online": <http://www.natcom.org/ctronline/nonverb.htm>.

Writing Follow-up   (page 26)

For students choosing Question 1: An example of a "case study" reflecting a misunderstanding due to cultural variations in the use of personal space can be seen in paragraphs 1, 2, and 5 of "Where Do We Stand?"

Students choosing Question 3 should be referred to pages 214–215 in the Student's Book for a review of summarizing.

CORE READING 3 (pages 27–31)
Time Talks, with an Accent Robert Levine

In this narrative essay, Levine discusses cultural differences in concepts of time and the intercultural conflicts and misunderstandings that often arise from these temporal variations. Focusing on his experiences as a visiting professor at a university in Brazil, he describes the difficulties he had adjusting to a new sense of social time that reflects different cultural values and beliefs than he was accustomed to in the United States. In order to enhance the intercultural experience, Levine stresses the importance of learning the unwritten rules about time in a new culture.

Main Ideas (page 31)

1 Social (versus clock) time is a culture's temporal orientation reflecting unconscious values, beliefs, and rules (pars. 14–15). The components of social time are concepts of punctuality; pace of life; and orientation to past, present, and future (par. 15).

2 Adjusting to a foreign concept of time is difficult because it reflects values, beliefs, and rules that are often very different from those of the visitor's culture and that are unwritten or hidden. "There is no dictionary to define these rules of time for them [children], or for strangers who stumble over the maddening incongruities between the time sense they bring with them and the one they face in a new land" (par. 15).

3 In the excerpt "Time Talks, with an Accent," Robert Levine maintains that there are cultural differences in concepts of time, reflecting diverse values and beliefs, which often lead to intercultural conflict and misunderstanding. By learning about a new culture's pace of life; rules of punctuality; and orientation to past, present, and future, a visitor can minimize problems and facilitate cultural adjustment.

Reflecting on Content (pages 31–32)

1 Levine means that rules of punctuality are strongly shaped by a culture's values and beliefs. A culture's concept of time reflects values and assumptions about social relationships (individualistic versus group-oriented), the relationship of people to nature (harmonious versus controlling), and social activity (doing versus being). The values that Althen discusses in the first core reading "American Values and Assumptions" such as individualism, privacy, competition, and an orientation toward achievement and action heavily influence a culture's orientation to time.

2 When Edward Hall refers to rules of social time as a silent language, he means that concepts of time are largely unwritten, hidden, ingrained, and, "like the air we breathe, so taken for granted that they are rarely discussed or even articulated" (par. 14). For similarities between verbal and nonverbal communication (including the use of time), see the comments on *Reflecting on Content* Question 1 on pages 5–6 of this manual.

3 Feelings that Levine experienced while encountering cultural differences in perceptions of time include distress (par. 3), panic (par. 5), franticness (pars. 5–6), enjoyment (par. 7), surprise (par. 8), confusion (par. 12), anger (par. 13), frustration (par. 14), and fascination (pars. 14, 16).

A Writer's Technique: *Supporting Details* (page 32)

1 The main idea all the anecdotes illustrate is that cultural differences exist in concepts of time, and this can lead to intercultural conflict and

misunderstanding. Brazilians tend to have a casual attitude toward time, where plans are fluid, schedules are easily changed, people always have time to see others, many things are done at the same time, and there is not a great concern with promptness. In contrast, the majority of those living in the United States generally see time as a limited commodity not to be wasted, value schedules and promptness, try to stick with original plans, are more concerned with accomplishing things than interacting with other people, and do one thing at a time.

2 Students usually find Levine's personal anecdotes an engaging way to illustrate his thesis. Since this is a personal, narrative mode of writing, students generally see less need for other types of support such as facts, statistics, and primary and secondary sources. Perceptive readers, however, point out that Levine does include types of support other than personal anecdote, including quotation (par. 2), definition (par. 4), and source citation (par. 15).

Vocabulary: *Guessing Meaning from the Context*   (pages 32–33)

Following are synonyms for the five vocabulary items: 1 *unwavering:* unchanging, unhesitating, resolute 2 *a piece of cake:* easy, simple, uncomplicated 3 *shuffling:* shifting, moving, rearranging 4 *intertwined:* interwoven, interlaced, united 5 *volatile:* intense, extreme, explosive

Discussion   (page 34)

1 When discussing attitudes toward punctuality, students may want to refer to the *Previewing the Topic* activity on page 26 of their text. In time perception, an orientation to the past, as found in most East Asian cultures, stresses the value of history, tradition, custom, and heritage. An orientation to the present, as is common in Latin American cultures, stresses that the moment is most important – that the future is vague and unknowable and that what is real is in the here and now. An orientation to the future, prevalent in English-speaking cultures, emphasizes future activities and accomplishments and the fact that the future is grander and more rewarding than the past or present.

2 The questionnaire should deal with the general pace of life, attitudes toward punctuality, and orientation to past, present, and future. Students might include questions relating to intercultural conflicts and misunderstandings.

3 All three Web broadcasts feature Robert Levine, author of "Time Talks, with an Accent," discussing cultural differences in perceptions of time. The first broadcast is a short interview with Levine. The second two are longer call-in talk shows with other featured guests in addition to Levine.

Writing Follow-up (page 34)

Students choosing Question 3 should be referred to pages 214–215 in the Student's Book for a review of summarizing.

MAKING CONNECTIONS (page 35)

1 The origin of the intercultural tensions that all the authors discuss is cultural differences in values, beliefs, perceptions, and behaviors, including verbal and nonverbal communication.

2 All three authors state or imply that an awareness of cultural differences is essential in minimizing intercultural conflict, misunderstanding, and stereotyping. Moreover, an awareness of one's own ethnocentrism (culturally determined values and perceptions) is important in avoiding problems and facilitating intercultural communication.

3 The larger conversational distance in the United States and Northern Europe than in the Mediterranean, Middle East, and South America (pars. 7–8) reflects a greater emphasis on individualism and privacy. Eye contact in the United States (pars. 6, 11) reflects the values of directness and assertiveness. The Japanese greeting involving bowing indicates the importance of formality in that culture as opposed to the less formal greetings common in the United States and Arab countries (par. 15).

4 The values of individualism; privacy; the future, change, and progress; and achievement, action, work, and materialism all shape the prevalent time orientation in the United States that Levine discusses: the fast pace of life, stress on punctuality, and orientation to the future.

5 Althen's use of supporting detail includes personal anecdote (pars. 4–6), example (pars. 14–15, 21–23, 33, 39, 44), quotation (pars. 23, 30, 32, 38, 40), citation of a primary source (par. 18), and citation of a secondary source (par. 9). Davis uses anecdote (par. 1), example (pars. 5, 7–8, 11, 15), quotation (pars. 1, 6, 10, 12, 15), and citation of sources. The individuals mentioned in paragraphs 6–7, 10, 14–16, and 17–18 represent a mixture of primary and secondary sources that are often not spelled out due to the popular readership of the article. Levine's use of supporting detail includes personal anecdote (pars. 5–7, 10–13), quotation (par. 2), definition (par. 4), and source citation. The individuals mentioned in paragraphs 2 and 15 represent a primary and a secondary source that are not documented due to the nonacademic audience.

ADDITIONAL READING 1 (pages 36–39)

Polite but Thirsty Yaping Tang

In this narrative essay, Tang describes the culture shock that she and many of her Chinese students experienced when confronting new codes, values, and behaviors in the United States. Tang focuses on cross-cultural differences between the United States and China, especially in verbal communication style. She discusses reasons for her bilingual students' culture shock and ways to facilitate adjustment to a new culture.

In addition to its thematic content, the essay may be used to help develop the writing technique introduced in the chapter: explaining and illustrating ideas with supporting detail. Students can identify Tang's main points and the details she uses to support them, including personal anecdote (par. 5), quotation (pars. 2, 5–7), examples (pars. 4–8), statistics (par. 1), and definition (par. 10).

Taking Notes While You Read (page 36)

Cross-cultural differences in values between the United States and China include informality/formality (par. 4), equality/social hierarchy (par. 4), directness/indirectness (pars. 5–7), and self-assertiveness/modesty (par. 6).

After You Read (page 39)

For students choosing Question 1: Tang's main point is that newcomers to a culture – with a different history, geography, language, and system of values, beliefs, and behaviors – typically experience culture shock, or psychological disorientation. Through the process of adapting to a new environment, however, newcomers can broaden their perspectives and gain insight into themselves and the world around them.

ADDITIONAL READING 2 (pages 40–43)

Friends and Strangers Margaret K. (Omar) Nydell

In this chapter excerpt, Nydell examines cultural differences between Arab and Western concepts of friendship and the intercultural conflicts and misunderstandings that often arise from varying relational expectations and obligations. Since the chapter comes from a book that is designed as a guide for Western sojourners to Arab cultures, Nydell provides advice on negotiating friendships and avoiding relational damage, especially in the areas of giving and receiving favors, introducing oneself, and visiting others.

In addition to its thematic content, this reading may be used to help develop the writing technique of the chapter: main ideas and supporting details. Students can identify Nydell's main points and the details she uses to support them, including anecdotes (pars. 5, 6, 16, 18), examples (pars. 4, 9, 12, 15, 17), quotations (pars. 10, 16, 17, 19), and source citation (par. 19).

Cross-cultural differences between Arab and Western concepts of friendship include the following:

- Arab: A friend is someone whose company one enjoys and whose duty is to give help and do favors to the best of his or her ability (par. 2). Westerner: A friend is someone whose company one enjoys but whom one doesn't expect to have the same sense of duty (par. 2).

- Arab: One never openly refuses a request from a friend (par. 4). Westerner: It is acceptable to refuse a request from a friend (par. 5).

- Arab: An oral promise has its own value as a response (par. 7). Westerner: Actions are valued more than words (par. 7).

- Arab: One expects loyalty from a friend (par. 11). Westerner: One doesn't expect the same sense of loyalty (par. 11).

- Arab: When introducing oneself, it is common to give a lot of information about oneself, one's family, and one's social connections (par. 12). Westerner: When introducing oneself, one discloses less personal information (par. 12).

- Arab: One visits one's friends often and has little concern about privacy (par. 15). Westerner: One visits one's friends less often and has a strong sense of privacy (par. 19).

- Arab: One expects a friend to reciprocate invitations (par. 17). Westerner: One doesn't have as strong a need for reciprocal invitation (par. 17).

After You Read (page 43)

For students choosing Question 1: Nydell's main point is that there are striking differences in concepts of friendship between the Western and Arab world and that these variations often lead to intercultural conflict and misunderstanding. In order to avoid problems and damage to personal relationships when visiting an Arab culture, it is important for Westerners to be aware of the expectations and obligations inherent in Arab definitions of friendship.

ADDITIONAL READING 3 (pages 44–51)

A Coward Premchand

This short story by a prominent Indian author focuses on the relationship between a young woman and man from different castes. Both individuals maintain that they are ready to defy their families and the cultural prohibition on intercaste marriage, accepting the "new ways," but, in the end, the man backs down, and the woman, crestfallen and shamed, takes her own life.

Before discussing the message of the story, instructors might start by asking students what they think the narrative has to do with the theme of the chapter: intercultural communication. Students usually mention the two reasons the story was included in this chapter: (1) the focus on *intracultural* differences in values, beliefs, and behaviors (the differences between cultural groups in a particular country are often as great or greater than differences between countries), and (2) the focus on different types of *conflict* – a major issue in the study of intercultural communication. The story often reminds students of similar tragic love stories in their own culture and leads to discussions of individual choice versus social and family obligations, tradition versus change, arranged versus "love" marriages, and cultural differences in perceptions of suicide.

Taking Notes While You Read   (page 44)

Conflicts in the story include those between Prema and Keshav, Prema and her parents, Keshav and his parents, Prema's and Keshav's fathers, Prema's mother and father, female and male, caste and caste, younger and older generation, individual and society, tradition and new ideas, illusion and reality, fate and free will, courage and cowardice, arranged marriage and love marriage, shame and honor, and honesty and dishonesty.

After You Read   (page 51)

For students who choose Question 1, the main theme is the conflict between the old caste customs and the new ways (pars. 1, 17, 36, 44, 55). The central message might read: "One must follow the dictates of one's own conscience, even if it means going against one's family and long-standing cultural traditions" or "The rigid caste system in India must give way to a less restrictive society that provides people with equal opportunities and allows for individual choice in such matters as marriage."

ADDITIONAL READING 4 (page 51)
The Blind Men and the Elephant John Godfrey Saxe

As an in-class activity, students might read the well-known Hindu fable in a small group and then write a moral in poetic or prose form. After sharing their morals, students can compare them with the message of the final two stanzas that were deleted from the original. The fable makes a nice concluding activity for a unit on intercultural communication since it reflects many of the issues raised in the other selections in this chapter.
    The last two stanzas of the original fable are as follows:

> And so these men of Indostan
>   Disputed loud and long,
> Each in his own opinion
>   Exceeding stiff and strong

Though each was partly in the right,
    And all were in the wrong!

So oft in theologic wars,
    The disputants, I ween,
Rail on in utter ignorance
    Of what each other mean,
And prate about an Elephant
    Not one of them has seen!

    Some possible morals of the fable are the value of cultural relativity versus
absolute truth, the value of multiculturalism, and a warning against ethnocentrism
and stereotyping. Further morals include the danger of overconfidence and
being convinced one knows the truth, the need to develop a sense of humility,
the need to be flexible and open-minded, and the need to develop a tolerance
for ambiguity. The need to withhold judgment until one has all the facts, the
danger of trusting first impressions, the need for people to work together to
solve a problem, and the danger of mistaking the part for the whole (not being
able to see the forest for the trees) are additional morals of the fable.

ADDITIONAL READING 5 Humor

Presidents and Gifts (pages 53–54)

Condon and Yousef use this probably apocryphal anecdote, "Presidents and
Gifts," to illustrate differences between private and utilitarian property values.
President Kennedy represents the private value orientation common in North
America, where property is viewed as a right and almost an extension of the self.
In contrast, the Mexican leader has a utilitarian orientation, more common in
Latin America, where property is seen as having value only insofar as it is useful
and used.

Hägar the Horrible Cartoon Dik Browne (page 54)

Students might be asked to relate this cartoon to the concepts of time, including
punctuality, discussed in Levine's essay "Time Talks, with an Accent." (See the
comments for Question 3, *Reflecting on Content*, on page 8 of this manual.)

Education

The theme of this chapter is educational goals, practices, and problems. The readings and activities explore such issues as concepts of intelligence, use of the Internet in writing papers, multicultural education, and the qualities of good teachers.

The writing technique in the chapter involves identifying purpose and audience. In addition to working with students on this skill within the context of chapter readings, instructors should help students discover the ways in which identifying their own purpose and audience can help shape the content, organization, and style of their writing.

CORE READING 1 (pages 59–63)
School Is Bad for Children John Holt

In the first half of this provocative essay, Holt discusses his criticisms of formal education in the United States. He maintains that after years of miseducation, students lose their natural curiosity, confidence, energy, and resourcefulness. They become passive, lazy, indifferent nonlearners, with little sense of their own competence and worth. In the second half of the essay, Holt makes a number of recommendations to better address the needs and concerns of students and to enhance real learning.

This reading usually results in an engaging discussion of the goals of education, the pros and cons of formal education, and effective methods of teaching and learning. Many students from more traditional educational systems agree with Holt's major criticisms but feel that he overstates his points.

Main Ideas (page 63)

1 Holt's major criticisms of schools include the following:
   * Schools convert students' natural intelligence, curiosity, confidence, resourcefulness, independence, patience, and energy (pars. 1–2) into passiveness, laziness, dependence, indifference, boredom, and low self-esteem (pars. 2–5).
   * They discourage experimentation, creativity, and originality (par. 1).

- They teach students that "learning is separate from living" (par. 2), that students "cannot be trusted to learn and [are] no good at it" (par. 2), and that "learning is a passive process" (par. 2).
- They neglect students' needs and interests and show no respect for individual differences (par. 3).
- They teach students that "to be wrong, uncertain, confused, is a crime" (par. 4), and as a result, students start to "dodge, bluff, fake, cheat" (par. 4).
- They teach students not to interact with other people (par. 5) and to "live without paying attention to anything going on" around them (par. 6).
- They are almost always "ugly, cold, inhuman" (par. 6).
- They encourage dishonesty, suspicion, and anxiety (par. 7).
- They provide little opportunity for students to learn about the real world (pars. 10–11).

2 Holt's major recommendations for improving schools include the following:
- Abolish or modify compulsory school attendance (pars. 8–9).
- Take students into the community to learn about the real world firsthand (par. 10).
- Bring more of the real world into schools, including people from different professions, to talk about what they actually do (par. 11).
- Encourage students to work together and learn from each other (par. 12).
- Encourage students to learn to evaluate their own work and detect their mistakes and correct them (par. 13).
- Eliminate grades, exams, and marks (par. 13).
- Abolish the fixed, required curriculum (par. 14).

3 In the essay "School Is Bad for Children," John Holt argues that formal education damages students by converting their natural curiosity, energy, confidence, and creativity into passiveness, laziness, indifference, and low self-esteem. In order for true learning to take place in schools and for students to retain their originality and childlike sense of wonder, certain fundamental changes that encourage active learning and interaction with the real world must be made.

Reflecting on Content (page 63)

1 See paragraph 9, where Holt responds to common objections to abolishing compulsory school attendance.

2 Many people would probably argue that schools without school buildings would result in the fundamentals of education being neglected. How would students, for example, learn the "three Rs" (reading, writing, arithmetic) and other traditional subjects? How would they prepare themselves for entrance

to universities? How would they learn a sense of discipline and restraint if they were always running from one place to the next?

3 Students should consider the various reasons Holt gives for eliminating grades, exams, and marks (par. 13). They discourage active learning, originality, and creativity, and they encourage a sense of "being right" as the main objective of education. As a result, students learn "to dodge, bluff, fake, cheat" (par. 4), to be lazy, and to be dependent on the expert. Grades are useless since it is impossible to measure what a person really knows. Grades hinder real education (learning how to measure what one knows and does not know), and they are a waste of time for teachers.

A Writer's Technique: *Purpose and Audience* (page 64)

Identifying a writer's purpose and audience can be challenging for students. A discussion of these aspects of writing and their interrelationship enhances students' understanding of texts. In addition, it improves their ability to write essays by helping them clarify ideas and shaping content, organization, and style.

1 Holt has written this essay for several reasons: to provoke the reader to question traditional assumptions about education and its goals, curriculum, and teaching methods; to reflect on the ways in which formal education hinders personal growth, active learning, and interaction with the real world; and to consider improvements that will address the needs and concerns of students and enhance true learning.

2 After finishing the essay, the reader should think that traditional education negatively influences students' individual growth and learning in serious ways and that significant educational changes need to be made that take students' interests and needs into consideration. The audience should feel angry at the miseducation students have been receiving and motivated to help improve the situation.

3 Holt's audience – readers of *The Saturday Evening Post* – is a literate readership interested in social issues, including educational reform. Assuming that the audience is open to reconsidering traditional assumptions about education, Holt presents strong criticisms of formal education and controversial recommendations for improvement.

4 Most students feel that Holt is successful in outlining his criticisms of formal education and recommended changes. However, students also often feel that he overstates the negative aspects of traditional learning. Achieving one's purpose as a writer (in Holt's case, persuasion) involves a careful consideration of logical versus emotional presentation of ideas. Holt relies heavily on emotion and provocation in his attempt to convince his readers of the seriously flawed nature of formal education. Instructors might ask students to consider whether Holt has an effective balance of reason and emotion in his essay.

Vocabulary: *Synonyms* (pages 64–65)

Following are synonyms for the eight vocabulary items: 1 *in short:* in brief, in sum, in a word 2 *evaluation:* judgment, assessment, appraisal 3 *indifferent:* uninterested, apathetic, unconcerned 4 *trivial:* unimportant, insignificant, trifling 5 *abolish:* eliminate, do away with, get rid of 6 *compulsory:* mandatory, obligatory, required 7 *draw up:* formulate, design, prepare 8 *encounter:* experience, confront, face

Discussion (page 66)

1 See the comments for Questions 1 and 2 in *Main Ideas* on pages 15–16 of this manual.

2 When observing a class, students can consider such things as classroom practices (arrangement of seats, raising hands before asking questions, taking notes), activities (discussion, problem solving, small-group work), teaching methods (lecture, dialogue, audiovisual material), homework, classroom dynamics including ways in which teachers and students address each other, expression of personal opinion and disagreement, and so on. Instructors might ask students to consider the values and assumptions reflected in the classroom practices and activities such as those discussed in the first core reading of Chapter 1, "American Values and Assumptions."

3 The first broadcast is a panel discussion at Harvard Graduate School of Education on the pros and cons of standardized testing. The second broadcast is a short audio diary describing a teenage student's experience with home schooling.

Writing Follow-up (page 66)

Students choosing Question 3 should be referred to pages 214–215 in the Student's Book for a review of summarizing.

CORE READING 2 (pages 68–71)
How the Web Destroys the Quality of Students' Research Papers
David Rothenberg

In this personal persuasive essay, Rothenberg discusses the recent decline he's noticed in the quality of his students' writing, critical thinking, and original argumentation due to their increasing reliance on the World Wide Web as a research tool. In addition to outlining the educational hazards of the Web, Rothenberg stresses the responsibility of teachers to help develop students' critical thinking ability, including the hard work of reading closely, working through arguments, and assessing and synthesizing sources.

Although students often disagree with Rothenberg about the dangers of the Web research, finding him somewhat reactionary, they are engaged by the issues he discusses. This essay and the accompanying letter to the editor, "An Opposing View" by Richard Cummins, provide an opportunity for students to reflect on topics that are relevant to their academic success, including the nature of critical thinking; information versus knowledge; plagiarism; and locating, evaluating, and documenting library and Web sources.

Main Ides (page 72)

1 Rothenberg's criticisms of students' use of the World Wide Web for their writing research include the following:
- Decline in the quality of writing, critical thinking, and originality of thought (pars. 1–2, 4, 10, 12)
- Use of outdated sources that consist of articles and Web links but not in-depth commentaries found in books (pars. 3, 5)
- Use of unreliable sources (par. 5)
- Use of graphics that look impressive but often bear little relation to the paper topic (par. 4)
- Reliance on advertising for information versus real information (par. 6)
- Use of random, superficial research methods versus careful, analytical, logical work (pars. 6–9, 12) and synthesis of sources (pars. 4–5, 12)
- Laziness and decreased attention span (pars. 8, 13)
- Increased plagiarism (par. 10)
- Decline in use and quality of libraries (par. 11)
- Lack of time for revision of papers (par. 8) and reflection and acquisition of knowledge (par. 13)

2 Rothenberg believes that the decline in the quality of students' research papers is not only the fault of the students and the World Wide Web but of teachers. He states that he and other teachers need to spend more time teaching students how to read closely, think critically, and assess and synthesize sources (par. 12).

3 In the essay "How the Web Destroys the Quality of Students' Research Papers," David Rothenberg maintains that the quality of students' researched-based writing and original thought has been declining due to an excessive reliance by students on the World Wide Web – a medium that encourages quick, random research rather than assessment, analysis, and synthesis of print and electronic sources. The responsibility of improving students' writing lies both in the students themselves and in teachers, who need to help students develop their reading, critical thinking, and research abilities.

Reflecting on Content (page 73)

1 Students of college age, who have grown up with the Internet, tend to see Rothenberg as somewhat of a Luddite unwilling to accept technological change. They usually agree more with Cummins who, in his letter to the editor, suggests that Rothenberg overemphasizes the influence of the World Wide Web and falls victim to the common fallacy of blaming the medium instead of the ways it is used.

2 Students often agree that the random method of Web research that Rothenberg discusses reflects their own experience; they waste a lot of time looking at sites that aren't arranged in any order of importance. This question presents an opportunity for teachers to discuss effective Web research with students, including advanced searches that often generate more precise, useful results.

3 Rothenberg would likely maintain that Cummins is underestimating the influence of the World Wide Web, with which students have far more contact than the blackboard and overhead projector. Moreover, he would probably challenge the common notion that it's not the medium itself that is the problem but the ways in which it's used, contending that the acts of linking and networking on the Web are inherently random and, therefore, lead to "an ethereal randomness of thought" (par. 12) and a lack of logic and critical thinking.

A Writer's Technique: *Purpose and Audience* (page 73)

1 Rothenberg's major purpose is to convince the reader of the negative effects of the Web on students' writing and thinking and to suggest that the responsibility for improvement lies with the students, teachers, and educational administrators (pars. 10–11). He wants his audience to feel a sense of urgency in decreasing students' reliance on the Web for research and the need for teachers and administrators to help in the process. He would also like his readers to feel a sense of loss of originality and critical thinking in writing, a sense of loss of contact with books, and the need to recapture something that is rapidly disappearing.

2 Rothenberg's primary audience is college and university teachers and administrators – the central readership of *The Chronicle of Higher Education*. This audience informs Rothenberg's statements about the demise of college libraries (pars. 10–11) and the need for teachers to help improve students' writing and critical thinking (par. 12).

3 Most students feel that Rothenberg makes some valid points about the negative effects of the Web but that, as Holt does in the first core reading, he overstates his argument. Many teachers, in contrast, find Rothenberg right on target. Achieving one's purpose as a writer (in Rothenberg's case, persuasion) involves careful consideration of "logic and passion" (par. 12). Like Holt,

Rothenberg uses emotion and provocation in his attempt to convince his readers of the hazards of the Web. Students might be asked to consider whether Rothenberg has an effective balance of reason and emotion in his essay.

Vocabulary: *Parts of Speech* (pages 73–74)

A review of participial forms of descriptive adjectives can help students with this exercise: present participle (an *interesting* book, an *encouraging* teacher) and past participle (a *bored* child, a *worn* carpet).

Noun	Verb	Adjective	Adverb
brilliance	✳	**brilliant**	brilliantly
response	respond	responsive	responsively
decline	decline	declining	✳
virtuality	✳	**virtual**	virtually
perfectionist	perfect	perfect	perfectly
tact	✳	tactful	**tactfully**
fragment	fragment	**fragmented**	fragmentally
diversion	**divert**	diversionary	divertingly
rapidity	✳	rapid	**rapidly**
reason	**reason**	reasonable	reasonably
knowledge	know	knowledgeable	knowledgeably

Discussion (page 75)

1 See the comments for Question 1 in *Main Ideas* on page 19 of this manual.

2 This activity can often lead to an interesting discussion of types of plagiarism, reasons it is a serious offense, consequences, ways to avoid it, and differences in attitudes toward plagiarism across cultures. For a discussion of plagiarism and ways to avoid it, students may refer to page 132 in the Student's Book.

3 The first Web site includes evaluation checklists and sample sites for different types of Web pages. The criteria for evaluating all of these Web pages are the same: *authority, accuracy, objectivity, currency,* and *coverage.* The second Web site provides a checklist of the same five criteria for evaluating Web sources. For an additional checklist for evaluating both Internet and library sources, see page 126 in the Student's Book.

Writing Follow-up   (page 76)

Students choosing Question 2 might search for relevant library and Web sources in order to draft their statements about plagiarism. They should be careful, however, not to plagiarize any material!

CORE READING 3 (pages 77–83)
Multiple Intelligences and Emotional Intelligence David Miller Sadker and Myra Pollack Sadker

In this textbook excerpt directed at future teachers, the authors discuss traditional definitions and measurements of intelligence as reflected in IQ scores and the ways in which these concepts differ from those theories developed more recently by Howard Gardner (multiple intelligences) and Daniel Goleman (emotional intelligence). The authors outline Gardner's and Goleman's attempts to redefine and expand traditional concepts of intelligence in order to more accurately reflect the diverse nature of human capability. The authors also point out the fundamental questions that multiple intelligences and emotional intelligence raise about curriculum design, teaching methods, and assessment.

Students, especially those from more traditional education systems, may be unfamiliar with Gardner's and Goleman's unconventional theories of intelligence. It is hoped that these students will find these theories an engaging springboard to discuss such issues as definitions of intelligence, cross-cultural differences in conceptions of intelligence, IQ tests and other assessment tools, nature versus nurture, and goals of education including intellectual, emotional, and moral development.

Instructors may wish to use this excerpt as an example of APA documentation style. For an example of MLA source documentation style, see "Sex Roles" on pages 189–195 of the Student's Book.

Journal Writing   (page 76)

Students with a visual orientation may enjoy using the prewriting strategy *clustering* (see page 115 in the Student's Book), but other students find this technique less helpful. Students should be reminded that a visual sketch or map is just one of many prewriting strategies to explore and plan ideas. (Others are discussed on pages 113–118 of the Student's Book.) Students should be encouraged to experiment with a variety of techniques to see which they find most useful.

SAMPLE MATH PROBLEMS FOR IQ TEST   (page 78)

The answer to problem 1 is 5. (Add the numbers in the top row and subtract the number on the bottom.) The answer to problem 2 is 3. (Multiply the numbers in the top row and divide this by the number on the bottom.)

Students choosing Question 1 should see paragraphs 6–7 for examples of ways in which Gardner's multiple intelligences might influence curriculum design and assessment.

Main Ideas (page 83)

1 Gardner's concept of multiple intelligences (MI) and Goleman's concept of an emotional intelligence (EI) quotient differ from more traditional theories in the following ways:

- MI stresses a wide range of human abilities versus a more traditional focus on language and mathematical/logical skills (par. 2).
- MI and EI reflect a broad, flexible notion of human intelligence versus a fixed, permanent measurement of human ability (par. 5).
- MI and EI stress that interpersonal and intrapersonal abilities are as important a part of intelligence as linguistic and mathematical/logical skills.
- MI and EI emphasize different ways of assessing a person's diverse abilities such as portfolios and descriptive assessment (par. 7) versus traditional pencil-and-paper and IQ tests.
- MI provides a better explanation of why the quality of a person's performance may vary a lot in different activities rather than reflect a single standard of performance indicated by an IQ score (par. 5).
- EI is a better predictor of success than IQ (par. 8).
- MI stresses that specific aspects of intelligence vary cross-culturally versus a more traditional concept of universal intelligence (par. 5).

2 The authors mean that Gardner and Goleman have broadened concepts of human intelligence to reflect a greater range of abilities than those stressed in more traditional theories. This emphasis on diverse intelligences has profound implications for schools, including curriculum design, assessment, and teaching methods (pars. 6–7).

3 In the chapter excerpt "Multiple Intelligences and Emotional Intelligence," Myra Sadker and David Sadker explain Howard Gardner's and Daniel Goleman's recent attempts to redefine and expand traditional concepts of human intelligence in order to more accurately reflect the varying nature of human capability. The authors also stress the fundamental ways in which Gardner's multiple intelligences theory and Goleman's concept of emotional intelligence may inform curriculum design, instruction, and assessment.

Reflecting on Content (page 84)

1 Gardner's interpersonal and intrapersonal intelligences are quite similar to Goleman's concept of emotional intelligence. Both Gardner and Goleman

stress the importance of monitoring one's own and others' emotions, needs, and motivations.

2 When the authors say that emotional intelligence may be even more revolutionary than multiple intelligences theory, they mean that while multiple intelligences raises fundamental questions about curriculum and assessment, emotional intelligences may have relevance for a person's entire life, since it seems to be a reliable predictor of future success. That is, the radical reconception of traditional intelligence reflected in EQ theory has profound implications not only for school change but for the way one lives one's life.

3 Students usually enjoy completing the EQ assessment and comparing their scores. They should bear in mind, however, the authors' final statement when discussing the results of the assessment: "The students you will teach will learn in diverse ways, and a single IQ or even EQ score is unlikely to capture the range of their abilities and skills. . . ." (par. 10).

A Writer's Technique: *Purpose and Audience* (page 84)

1 The authors' purpose is to explain to future teachers how Gardner and Goleman have redefined and broadened conventional concepts of intelligence in order to more accurately reflect the diverse nature of human capability (par. 3). They also wish to inform readers of the profound implications that multiple intelligences and emotional intelligence have for their future careers as teachers, especially in the areas of curriculum design, instruction, and assessment. The authors stress that students have varying learning styles. Teachers are cautioned not to rely excessively on a single assessment tool (par. 10). The educational subject matter the authors discuss, the points they make about diverse concepts of intelligence, and the examples they give (pars. 6–8 and the sidebar "Where Do the Mermaids Stand?") are all relevant to the careers of future teachers.

2 Most students think that the authors discuss their topic clearly, provide interesting examples to support their points, and are successful in convincing readers of the limiting nature of traditional concepts of intelligence and the importance of multiple intelligences and emotional intelligence in expanding the range and diversity of educational ideas.

3 The purpose of the anecdote "Where Do the Mermaids Stand?" is to remind future teachers that some students will be "mermaids" – who are different and don't fit neatly into a category – and that educators need to think carefully about how to make room in their class for these nonconformists. The story relates to the reading in that it illustrates the diverse learning styles and intelligences of students and the need for teachers to accommodate this diversity in the classroom.

Vocabulary: *Antonyms*   (pages 84–85)

Following are antonyms for the eight vocabulary items: 1 *innate:* acquired, developed, learned 2 *broaden:* narrow, limit, constrict 3 *comprehensive:* incomplete, limited, restricted 4 *tangible:* intangible, immaterial, imperceptible 5 *competence:* incompetence, incapability, inability 6 *hold off:* proceed, continue, give in 7 *give in to:* resist, oppose, withstand 8 *topple:* support, maintain, uphold

Discussion   (page 86)

1 Students who come from traditional educational systems usually agree with Gardner about the heavy emphasis placed on language and mathematical-logical skills and test scores in assessing intelligence and academic competence (pars. 1–2). They don't generally find much stress on "the capacity to solve problems" (par. 2), curricular approaches that respond to diverse student abilities (par. 6), and comprehensive assessment tools such as portfolios and descriptive reports (par. 7). Although some students find educational value placed on Gardner's bodily-kinesthetic, musical, and spatial intelligences, they less often report the cultivation of interpersonal and intrapersonal intelligences or Goleman's emotional intelligence in the educational systems with which they are most familiar.

2 To help in the design of their lesson plan, students might review the educational approaches listed in paragraph 6 of the reading.

3 This "Multiple Intelligences Inventory" has sections corresponding to Gardner's list of multiple intelligences. Students indicate the relevance of statements relating to their personal lives, plot their scores for various intelligences on a bar graph, and determine the intelligence(s) in which they are strongest.

MAKING CONNECTIONS   (page 87)

1 Rothenberg advocates a more conventional approach to education than the other authors. He attacks the World Wide Web as an educational tool and stresses the importance of books and traditional library research (pars. 9, 13). Holt criticizes traditional school education and offers unconventional solutions to problems. Sadker and Sadker believe that traditional concepts of intelligence and methods of assessment are limiting. They stress the importance of unconventional theories of intelligence, such as multiple intelligences and emotional intelligences, which more accurately reflect the possibilities of which humans are capable (par. 3).

2 Holt blames formal education, including teachers, for students' "miseducation," which turns their natural curiosity and confidence into passivity and low self-esteem. For example, in paragraph 13, Holt speaks of

teachers who set themselves up as experts and correct students excessively instead of giving them a chance to detect their own mistakes. Holt implies that teachers need to do a better job of responding to their students' interests and needs and in fostering active, relevant learning. Similarly, Rothenberg implies that teachers bear much of the blame for their students' poor learning habits since they don't take enough time to help students develop their reading ability, critical thinking, and originality (par. 12).

3 Holt would likely agree with Gardner's multiple intelligences theory and certainly with the important role schools play in developing students' varying talents and abilities. For example, in paragraph 10, when Holt discusses the importance of students going out into the community and learning about the world first hand, he is implicitly stressing the need to develop students' diverse intelligences. In paragraphs 5 and 12, Holt emphasizes the importance of students interacting with each other (Gardner's interpersonal intelligence). In paragraph 13, Holt argues for better methods of assessment, including self-correction and the elimination of grades, exams, and marks (similar to Gardner's stress on holistic evaluation mentioned in par. 7). In the final paragraph, Holt asserts, "Children want . . . to make sense of the world, themselves, and other human beings." These are fundamental issues relating to existential intelligence.

4 Rothenberg would most likely not see the Internet as a good tool to develop Gardner's multiple intelligences. In the essay, Rothenberg criticizes the random nature of Web research versus careful analytical work (pars. 6–9, 12). This "hunt-and-peck" method of writing a paper (par. 8) and fragmented, superficial approach (par. 9) would not cultivate logical-mathematical or linguistic intelligence or develop students' writing. Cutting and pasting graphics into a paper with little relation to the subject (par. 4) would do little to enhance spatial intelligence. And the lack of time for reflection that leads to true knowledge (par. 13) would do little to foster interpersonal, intrapersonal, or existential intelligence.

5 All three readings are a type of persuasive writing. Each aims to convince the reader to believe something or to take a certain course of action. All three authors try to convince the reader of the limitations of certain educational approaches; of the need to enhance students' varying abilities; of the importance of active, student-centered learning; and of the need to reflect on the ways in which curriculum design, teaching methods, and assessment might be improved. Unlike Holt's and Rothenberg's persuasive essays, which are urgent in tone, Sadker and Sadker's piece is a textbook excerpt, with a more neutral tone and an informative intent. Yet, from the pedagogical approaches mentioned in paragraph 6 of the last reading, the sidebar "Where Do the Mermaids Stand?" and the positive statements about Gardner and Goleman in the final paragraph, it is clear that Sadker and Sadker are promoting an approach to education that emphasizes the development of

students' diverse abilities, not simply those that are refined by traditional methods.

ADDITIONAL READING 1 (pages 88–92)
The Teacher Who Changed My Life Nicholas Gage

In this personal essay, Gage paints a vivid picture of the seventh-grade English teacher who inspired him to pursue a career in journalism. The positive tone of this reading about a Greek war refugee who immigrates to the United States contrasts with the more critical tone of the first two core readings in the chapter. This essay may stimulate discussion about students' favorite and least favorite teachers, cultural differences in relationships between teachers and students, opportunities that education provides, the American Dream, and bilingual education.

After You Read (page 92)

For students choosing Question 1: Gage learns many important things from Miss Hurd. He learns the value of diligence and hard work (par. 6), journalism skills (par. 7), the logic and structure of the English language (par. 7), Greek literature (par. 7), and the power of the written word (par. 12).

For students choosing Question 2: Gage finds Miss Hurd an inspirational teacher for numerous reasons. She has students read stories about real people, especially underdogs, doing extraordinary things (par. 7). She introduces him to Greek literature, which provides a new perspective on, and pride in, his native country. She challenges him to confront the painful memories of his mother's death and his own escape from Communist guerrillas (pars. 9–10). She publishes his essay in the school newspaper and submits it to a contest, for which he wins a medal (par. 11). She attends his family celebrations, participates enthusiastically, and provides moral support (pars. 15, 17–20). Finally Miss Hurd encourages students, especially those from troubled homes, with "tough love."

ADDITIONAL READING 2 (pages 93–95)
Let's Tell the Story of All America's Cultures Ji-Yeon Mary Yuhfill

In a manner similar to the previous reading, this personal essay describes the educational experiences of an immigrant to the United States. Writing at the age of twenty-one, Yuhfill, a Korean-American student, bemoans the lack of discussion of people of color throughout her primary and secondary education, in both her classes and history books. She describes the discrimination and feeling of invisibility she experienced as a minority student. Yuhfill stresses the importance of a multicultural education that records the diverse histories and accomplishments of nonwhite Americans and provides students with a critical perspective on the discrepancies between the democratic ideals of the United States and its social realities.

Yuhfill's essay often leads to discussions of educational goals, the value of a multicultural education, the nature of students' own education (including the presence and lack of certain subjects and groups of people in history texts and classroom discussions), the American Dream, and ways to combat discrimination.

After You Read   (page 95)

For students choosing Question 1: Yuhfill's purpose in writing the essay is to convince her readers of the need for a multicultural curriculum. It should value the traditions and accomplishments of diverse groups of people and provide a critical perspective on the inconsistencies between the ideals and the social realities of the United States.

ADDITIONAL READING 3 (pages 96–97)

Coyote and the Crying Song Retold by Harold Courlander

This Hopi folktale is a powerful commentary on, or parable of, the learning process. Students might read the fable in class and then, in small groups, discuss what it has to say about education in general and the ways in which people learn and fail to learn.

Following is a list of possible educational lessons relating to "Coyote and the Crying Song." These lessons are similar in many ways to those of the Hindu fable, "The Blind Men and the Elephant," on pages 52–53 in the Student's Book.

- Coyote is overconfident (par. 5). His arrogance and narrow-mindedness obstruct real learning.

- Coyote thinks in a simple, rigid, linear manner (pars. 5, 9). He needs to develop a sense of nonlinear (metaphorical) thinking.

- The only type of learning Coyote knows is memorization and recitation (pars. 9–10). This does not help him negotiate difficult situations. Education should de-emphasize memorization and purely verbal learning and stress creativity, experimentation, and learning in the real world.

- Coyote is very impatient and gets frustrated easily (pars. 10, 19). This hinders real learning, which takes time and effort.

- Coyote rushes into things and doesn't pay attention to what's going on around him. He doesn't know the meaning of the proverb "Look before you leap."

- Coyote gets very upset when he makes a mistake (pars. 10, 19). He needs to learn that making mistakes is not a crime but a part of learning.

- Coyote (the student) expects the dove (his teacher) to tell him what to do: "You must give it [the song] to me again" (par. 11). Coyote needs to be more self-reliant and to show more initiative.
- Coyote (the student) doesn't listen to the dove (his teacher). The dove says she is crying and not singing (par. 4), but Coyote doesn't care. Coyote needs to be more attentive and respectful.
- The dove (the teacher) isn't trying new approaches to help Coyote (the student) learn. The dove doesn't really listen to Coyote.
- Coyote might be seen as a teacher and the dove as a student. The teacher doesn't listen to the dove but just orders the student around.

ADDITIONAL READING 4 (pages 98–99)
First Grade – Standing in the Hall Cheryl Savageau

Students may have experienced learning problems and school punishments similar to those encountered by the boy in the poem. Some students find Savageau's message about respect for students of all backgrounds and abilities very moving. The poem often stimulates discussion about educational issues including literacy, oral versus written traditions, bilingual education, minority students, learning problems and disabilities, student punishment, and ways that students learn and fail to learn.

After You Read (page 99)

For students choosing Question 1: Savageau points out four educational needs: The need for teachers to consider students as individuals with varying concerns, interests, and abilities; to respect students of varying educational and ethnic backgrounds; to vary their pedagogical approach to accommodate students' diverse learning styles and challenges; and to foster the self-esteem, creativity, and personal voice of their students (the "song" in line 31). Savageau also warns of the danger of self-fulfilling prophecies, where students come to believe the negative comments made about their character and ability, and the destructive potential of traditional types of punishment (such as standing in the hall), especially for those with learning difficulties.

ADDITIONAL READING 5 Humor
The Test (pages 99–100)

Students usually enjoy this joke, which leads to discussions of grading policies, study habits, partying, and cheating and punishments if caught.

Life in Hell Cartoon Matt Groening (page 100)

Instructors might ask students to relate the cartoon to educational issues raised in the chapter readings, especially to Holt's criticisms of schools in "School Is Bad for Children." (See the comments for *Main Ideas* in Question 1 on pages 15–16 of this manual.)

Mass Media and Technology

The focus of this chapter is the positive and negative influences of mass media and other forms of technology, including the Internet, e-mail, and television. The readings and activities explore such issues as the limits and possibilities of technology, advertising techniques, and the ethics of downloading music from the Internet.

The writing technique in the chapter introduces the use of similes and metaphors as figures of speech. In addition to working with students on this skill within the context of chapter readings, instructors should encourage students to use figurative language to make their own writing lively and memorable.

CORE READING 1 (pages 137–144)
Computers and the Pursuit of Happiness David Gelernter

In this argumentative essay, Gelernter addresses three questions: (1) whether, thanks to computers and the Internet, we are now living in a new information age, (2) whether computers have been beneficial or detrimental to humanity over the last 50 years, and (3) whether computers are likely to have a positive or negative influence over the next half century. Gelernter attempts to answer these questions through historical comparisons. He concludes that we are not living in a revolutionary information age. Computers have not made people any happier on the whole, and computer technology will not contribute significantly to our well-being in the future.

Gelernter's provocative essay and the accompanying letter to the editor, "An Opposing View" by Winn F. Martin, sometimes lead to engaging discussions of the functions and effects of the mass media and other forms of technology. Additional discussion themes include the possibilities and limitations of technology, the nature of technological change, the pros and cons of the Internet, online shopping and education, the difference between information and knowledge, and the distinction between reality and virtual reality.

For another piece dealing with the negative effects of the Internet and a countering letter to the editor, students may be referred to Rothenberg's article in Chapter 2, "How the Web Destroys the Quality of Students' Research Papers" (pages 68–72).

31

Main Ideas (page 144)

1 Gelernter answers the first question negatively: We are not living in a new information age and computers and the Internet do not represent a revolutionary development in human history except in science and engineering (pars. 2, 12). He disputes the claims of those arguing the existence of a new information age (pars. 5–9). Gelernter also answers the second question negatively: Despite the information and wealth that computers have generated, human happiness hasn't increased on the whole (par. 19). New technologies have come into existence, but the social structures they've engendered haven't necessarily improved (par. 20), and the human element associated with the old structures has decreased (par. 23). Finally, Gelernter answers the third question by stating that technology will have little to do with human happiness in the future (pars. 22, 37). Despite the new possibilities that novel technologies introduce (par. 28), human uniqueness and, ultimately, happiness lie beyond technological strength, speed, and intellect (pars. 36–37).

2 Gelernter means that, instead of just looking at what a new technology can do and how it is better than an old one, it is more important to be aware of the new social structure that the technology creates and whether it represents an improvement. For example, many technological innovations have taken place, such as online shopping and education, but the human ingredient associated with the old social structure has often diminished (par. 23).

3 In his essay, "Computers and the Pursuit of Happiness," David Gelernter argues that we are not currently living in a new information age, that computers have not increased human happiness in the past, and that computer technology and the Internet will not contribute to the pursuit of happiness in the future. Instead of automatically regarding a new technology as an improvement over an old one, it is more important to consider the new social structure that the technology creates, which often decreases the human element of the old structure.

Reflecting on Content (page 144)

1 Students often disagree with Gelernter's contention that we are not living in a new information age and that computers and the Internet do not represent a revolutionary development in human history (par. 2). They usually point to the information technologies that Gelernter mentions in paragraph 6 and argue that most people today have more contact with the Internet than they ever had with the other technologies, except for television. Having grown up with computers and the Internet, students usually believe that these information and communications technologies have contributed significantly to their personal welfare and to society in general. They tend not to reflect very often on the potential downside of the technologies, especially the new, often less personalized social structures they have engendered (pars. 20–24).

2 Most students tend to agree with Winn's critique of Gelernter's argument, especially the charge that he is a Luddite who naively underestimates the influence of the Internet as a person-to-person communications medium that will increasingly enhance global education and democracy (pars. 3–4 of Winn's letter).

3 Gelernter provides several types of evidence to support his points: historical examples (pars. 3, 6, 8–9, 21–22, 24), contemporary examples (pars. 4, 12–13), imagined examples (pars. 29–30), quotations (pars. 7, 10, 27–29), source citations (pars. 7, 27), and personal experience (pars. 13, 18–19, 34). Students generally find Gelernter's extensive use of supporting detail effective, although they often fault the parallel he makes between computer technology and the Industrial Revolution (pars. 3, 5, 8, 28).

A Writer's Technique: *Figures of Speech*   (page 145)

Students, even quite advanced ones, often have difficulty understanding figurative language. Gelernter's colorful use of figures of speech throughout the essay may present a challenge to students. This activity helps students understand the similes and metaphors that Gelernter uses and the reasons he uses them. (For other examples of figurative language, see pars. 11, 23, 29, 36.)

1 Figure of Speech: Metaphor
   Comparison: Computers and light snow
   Main Idea: Computer technology makes things look different on the surface, but in reality, its information functions are no different from those of the past.

2 Figure of Speech: Metaphor
   Comparison: Computer revolutions and icebergs
   Main Idea: The computer revolution may seem real and impressive, but in most areas it has not actually occurred yet.

3 Figure of Speech: Simile
   Comparison: The World Wide Web and plumbing
   Main Idea: The Web improves the speed at which we receive information but makes no improvement in the ultimate quality of what we get.

4 Figure of Speech: Metaphor
   Comparison: Future technology and a candy store
   Main Idea: In the future, humanity will take delight in all sorts of modern technologies.

5 Figure of Speech: Simile
   Comparison: Computer technology and the Eiffel Tower
   Main Idea: Computers are generating novel possibilities and structures.

Vocabulary: *Phrasal Verbs* (page 146)

1 *to blow up:* to cause something to explode
2 *to add up:* to consider all the advantages and disadvantages of something in order to form an opinion about it
3 *to dream up:* to think of a plan or an idea, especially one that seems unusual or strange
4 *to size up:* to think about a situation or person in order to form a judgment or opinion about them
5 *to trade in:* to give as part of the payment for something new
6 *to tune in:* to access, listen to, or watch (for example, a radio or television program)
7 *to usher in:* to introduce or cause something new to start
8 *to toss out:* to throw out or discard

Discussion (page 147)

1 Students might consider the following technologies and the pros and cons of the social structures that they have created: automobiles, clocks, electric motors, cell phones, digital cameras, computers, the Internet, television, and video games.

2 Depending on the time available, this debate can be conducted spontaneously, after some classroom preparation, or after substantive preparation out of class.

3 The first broadcast is a panel discussion of the pros and cons of the PC revolution. The second broadcast is a panel discussion of the largely negative influence of pop culture on children – including violence and sex in the media – and what can be done about it.

CORE READING 2 (pages 149–153)
We've Got Mail – Always Andrew Leonard

In this personal essay, Leonard discusses the advantages and disadvantages of e-mail and other forms of online communication, especially in terms of the ways people interact with each other. Maintaining that the Internet is a revolutionary technological development (something Gelernter disputes in the first core reading), Leonard traces the history of its most popular application – e-mail – and the ways this new communications medium may be seen as a Devil's bargain, facilitating yet complicating people's lives.

Most students, having grown up in a wired world, tend to see the Web and e-mail as media that have only influenced their lives in positive ways. This essay is helpful in encouraging students to think about the ways in which the Internet might affect their lives negatively in both a personal and social manner.

Journal Writing (page 148)

One of the most common prewriting techniques to generate and organize ideas is *brainstorming* – making a list of everything that comes to mind when one thinks about a topic and then arranging the ideas into categories. Instructors might remind students that brainstorming is just one of many prewriting strategies to explore and plan ideas. Others are discussed on pages 113–118 of the Student's Book. Instructors should encourage students to experiment with a variety of techniques to see which they find most useful.

Main Ideas (page 154)

1 Leonard mentions several contradictions in the essay: e-mail saves and wastes time (par. 4); it simplifies and complicates life (par. 4) and is convenient and inconvenient (par. 4); it brings people together and pushes them apart (par. 4); e-mail contributes to the fast pace of life and allows people to cope with it (par. 5); it increases and decreases literacy (par. 13); e-mail represents a vast historical archive but one that is unstable (par. 15); and finally, Leonard maintains that e-mail demolishes all boundaries, which may be either a blessing or a curse (par. 19).

2 Through the anecdote, Leonard is reinforcing his thesis: E-mail is both a blessing and a curse – a "Devil's bargain" (par. 19) in which we gain and lose something at the same time. E-mail gives us more control over our lives in certain ways but less control in others.

3 In his article "We've Got Mail – Always," Andrew Leonard maintains that e-mail and other forms of online communication influence people's lives positively and negatively, especially in terms of the ways they interact with each other. E-mail is both a blessing and a curse – a Faustian bargain in which we gain and give up something at the same time.

Reflecting on Content (page 154)

1 Leonard argues that e-mail is both a blessing and a curse, depending on how it's viewed. Online communication is a "Devil's bargain" (par. 19) in which we gain and lose something at the same time. Leonard ends the article with the statement: "E-mail doesn't just collapse distance, it demolishes all boundaries. And that can be, depending on the moment, either a blessing or a curse" (par. 19).

2 See paragraph 4, in which Leonard argues that e-mail brings people together and isolates them at the same time.

3 A Devil's, or Faustian, bargain is a situation in which one gains and loses something at the same time. It also implies something that is done for present gain without consideration of future cost or consequences. For an example of a Devil's bargain, see paragraph 21 of "Computers and the

Pursuit of Happiness" on pages 140–141 of the Student's Book, in which Gelernter compares modern plumbing and shared public wells. Also see the technologies listed under Question 1 in *Discussion* for Gelernter's article on page 34 of this manual.

A Writer's Technique: *Figures of Speech* (pages 154–155)

1 Comparison: E-mail and a lifeline (a rope used for saving or protecting someone)
   Main Idea: E-mail allowed me to stay connected with my dispersed family.

2 Comparison: E-mail and a lubricating substance
   Main Idea: E-mail facilitates social interaction and communication, but this may become extreme.

3 Comparison: Literacy and quicksand
   Main Idea: E-mail may not be enhancing literacy but contributing to its decline as people write in increasingly casual and simplistic ways.

4 Comparison: E-mail and an archive
   Main Idea: E-mail may provide a historical record of human communication.

5 Comparison: E-mail and an explosive substance
   Main Idea: E-mail destroys all boundaries between one's personal and social life.

Vocabulary: *Verb-Preposition Combinations* (page 155)

1 introduce into 2 cope with 3 interact with 4 worry over 5 border on
6 collaborate on 7 contribute to 8 refrain from

Discussion (page 156)

1 The first ten items in the chart on the following page are paired with their opposites. The other items do not have counterparts.

Benefits of Online Communication	Drawbacks of Online Communication
• saves time (par. 4)	• wastes time (par. 4)
• simplifies life (par. 4)	• complicates life (par. 4)
• increases control over one's life (par. 4)	• decreases control over one's life (par. 17)
• increases contact among people (par. 4)	• isolates people (par. 4)
• is convenient (par. 4)	• is inconvenient (par. 4)
• encourages real artists (par. 4)	• encourages con artists and crime (par. 4)
• saves money (par. 8)	• results in lost work through viruses (par. 15)
• increases literacy (par. 13)	• decreases literacy (par. 13)
• serves as an historical archive (par. 15)	• is fragile and unstable (par. 15)
• flattens hierarchies at work and enhances communication among workers and supervisors: social lubricant (pars. 11–12)	• encourages quick, casual, unthinking, uncreative responses; insults; and messages sent to wrong people (pars. 12–14)
• helps with job (pars. 3, 8, 18) • helps freedom fighters and conducting campaigns (par. 4) • helps authors write books (par. 4) • allows one to work at home (par. 8) • helps one balance home and work responsibilities (par. 8) • helps one transcend physical limitations (par. 9) • encourages shy people to date (par. 10) • enhances global collaboration (par. 16)	• encourages spam and pornography (pars. 2, 12) • encourages flame wars (par. 2) • decreases attention spans (par. 5) • increases reliance on new and quick stimulation (par. 5, 13) • encourages pop-culture triviality (par. 13) • may come back to haunt one (par. 15) • results in loss of distinction between work and play (par. 17)

2 Depending on the time available, this debate can either be conducted spontaneously, after some classroom preparation, or after substantial preparation out of class.

3 Both surveys ask questions relating to people's use of, and attitudes toward, the Internet. Another online questionnaire that may be used is the "Internet Addiction Test" found on the Web site of the Center for Online Addiction: <http://www.netaddiction.com/resources/internet_addiction_test.htm>. After taking the test, some students determine that they are indeed "online addicts" – an increasing occurrence among college students away from home for the first time.

CORE READING 3 (pages 158–165)

Propaganda Techniques in Today's Advertising Ann McClintock

In this textbook article, McClintock focuses on the propaganda techniques that advertisers and politicians use to influence people's opinions and to sell products, viewpoints, and candidates. McClintock argues that Americans are being brainwashed by advertising images and messages that flood their daily lives. She discusses seven propaganda tactics commonly used by advertisers and politicians, the ways in which they are effective in swaying opinion, and the need for consumers and voters to be aware of these manipulative techniques in order to maintain independent thought and action.

Students usually enjoy discussing the various propaganda techniques – advertisements, political rhetoric, and other forms of "brainwashing" in different cultures – and the ways in which persuasive tactics are used in the mass media, especially in magazine advertisements and TV commercials.

Journal Writing (page 157)

See the comments for Question 2 in *Discussion*, on pages 40–41 of this manual.

Main Ideas (page 165)

1 a. *name calling:* the use of negative names and labels applied to an opposing side or competitor in order to make the audience feel mistrustful, fearful, or angry. Name calling is an effective way of damaging the opposition by creating negative feelings in the audience (par. 5).

   b. *glittering generalities:* the use of attractive names and labels applied to a product or person in order to arouse positive feelings in the audience. Glittering generalities are an effective way of enhancing the image of a product or politician by creating affirmative feelings and connotations (pars. 6–8).

   c. *transfer:* the association of a product or person with a symbol that most people respect. Transfer is an effective way of enhancing the image of a product or point of view by fostering confidence in the viewer (pars. 9–11).

   d. *testimonial:* the endorsement of a product or person by a celebrity. One of the most popular advertising techniques, the testimonial takes advantage of the respect people have for a celebrity to make the product or politician stand out (pars. 12–15).

   e. *plain folks:* an appeal to the common person. Stressing that we're all in the same boat and just hardworking, everyday Joes, the plain folks technique is effective in fostering confidence and assuring people of the genuine quality of a product or person (pars. 16–17).

   f. *card stacking:* the suppression or distortion of information. Using half-truths, oversimplification of facts, and straw-man arguments, card stacking is often effective in swaying people's opinion and behavior (pars. 18–20).

  g. *bandwagon:* an appeal to people's desire to do what others are doing. Stressing that everyone else is doing or thinking the same thing, the bandwagon technique appeals to people's wish not to be different (pars. 21–22).

2 All of the propaganda techniques appeal to people's emotions – not their minds – and often capitalize on prejudices and biases (par. 23). These emotional appeals may be very effective in swaying people's opinions.

3 In the essay "Propaganda Techniques in Today's Advertising," Ann McClintock argues that Americans are being seduced and brainwashed, often willingly, by advertisers and politicians, who use various propaganda techniques to sell their products and points of view. By developing the ability, however, to think critically about the ways in which advertisers sway public opinion, people can combat the flood of propaganda messages in the mass media and maintain their independence of thought and behavior.

Reflecting on Content (page 166)

1 Students often maintain that all of the propaganda techniques are equally effective in influencing people's opinions due to their appeal to emotion and not to intellect. However, students typically argue that glittering generalities, transfer, and testimonials are especially effective due to their prevalence in the mass media. Some students point to card stacking as a particularly effective device because it is difficult to detect and combat (par. 18).

2 McClintock sees propaganda as a serious threat because it is so prevalent in the mass media (pars. 1, 3). Propaganda often appeals to emotions and prejudices (par. 23), it influences people's opinions and behavior subconsciously (par. 1), and people are often willing victims of brainwashing (pars. 1, 23). McClintock portrays propaganda as a highly effective "war" in which we are bombarded by advertising images in all forms of media and where "any tactic is considered fair" (pars. 2–3).

3 For examples of metaphors, see A *Writer's Technique: Figures of Speech,* below.

A Writer's Technique: *Figures of Speech* (page 166)

1 Comparison: Advertisers and seducers/brainwashers (also advertisers and guests)

  Main Idea: People are so strongly influenced by advertising messages in the media that they accept them without thinking.

2 Comparison: Propaganda and a war

  Main Idea: People are bombarded with advertising images in their daily lives.

3 Comparison: Name calling and a weapon directed at the enemy
  Main Idea: Name calling is a propaganda technique that attacks the opposing side or competitor with negative labels.

4 Comparison: General Electric and someone who restores life to something inanimate
  Main Idea: General Electric benefits people in many ways (electricity animates or energizes people's lives). Note the word play: General Electric animates life and also provides good things to people.

5 Comparison: Political ads and the American flag
  Main Idea: Political ads often appeal to people's sense of patriotism.

Vocabulary: *Connotations of Words* (pages 166–167)

Even quite advanced students find this exercise challenging. Instructors might stress to students that the study of connotations and denotations of words is important in their understanding of texts and communication of meaning as developing writers.

1 seduce 2 both equally negative 3 victim 4 propaganda 5 totalitarian
6 foreign (see the author's discussion of *foreign* and *imported* in par. 5 of the Student's Book) 7 boast 8 saccharine 9 bias 10 both equally negative

Discussion (page 168)

1 a. *plain folks* ("my fellow Americans," "my fellow citizens of the world"), *glittering generalities* ("citizens of the world," "freedom of man"), and *bandwagon* ("what together we can do").

   b. *glittering generalities* ("creative product," "higher humanity," "prototype"), *weasel words* ("almost exclusively"), and *card stacking* ("All the human culture, all the results of art, science, and technology that we see before us today, are almost exclusively the creative product of the Aryan.").

   c. *glittering generalities* ("Trident Advantage"), *transfer* ("Trident Advantage does something for teeth that milk does for bones"), *card stacking* ("up to 4 times" and "Recaldent, a revolutionary ingredient").

   d. *glittering generalities* ("American," "democracy," "proud way of life," "high in ideals and purpose," "Royalist cigars," "American Family," "fine in quality," "superb cigar-making experience," "a proud America"), *transfer* ("democracy," "Royalist"), and *bandwagon* ("American Family").

2 The Tempur-Pedic mattress advertisement on page 159 reflects the following propaganda techniques: (1) *name calling* ("dinosaur," "uncomfortable outmoded bed," "makes all other beds obsolete," "fancy on the outside"), (2) *glittering generalities* ("famous," "fabulous," "phenomenon," "marvel," "miracle," "perfect," "rave reviews"), (3) *transfer* ("you have a nice home . . .

drive a fine car . . . enjoy the good things of life"), (4) *testimonial* (NASA, U.S. Space Foundation, Space Awareness Alliance, sleep clinics, health professionals, TV, radio, magazines, newspapers), (5) *card stacking* (weasel words: "our technology is *recognized* by NASA . . . ," "it *selectively* adjusts"; unfinished claim: "cuts tossing and turning up to 83%"; vague claims: "millions have discovered," "our fabulous, fatigue-fighting, energy-elevating weightless sleep phenomenon," "marvel of molecular physics," "new weightless-sleep material," "thousands of sleep clinics"; and scientific-sounding claims: "anti-G-force research," "self-ventilating viscoelastic microcells"), and (6) *bandwagon* ("millions have discovered," "thousands of sleep clinics and health professionals"). Note also the contrast between the pictures (old versus new "mattress," inanimate versus animate, dog under the bed versus playing with the man), use of word play ("stop sleeping on a dinosaur," "Tempur-Pedic," "only one moving part – you"), and repeated use of "free" at the end to stimulate the reader's desire to try the product.

The Radisson Seven Seas Cruises advertisement on page 160 reflects the following propaganda techniques: (1) *glittering generalities* ("subtleties of Europe," "golden light of Tuscany," "enchant your ears," "spectacular," "luxury," "spacious stateroom," "gracious service," "fine cuisine," "qualities," "accolades," "rare delight"), (2) *transfer* (Sorrento red – a fine wine – and the cruise; "garden of Monet's colors"; "atop a medieval tower"; "spirited music of Barcelona"; and the ship names "Song of Flower," "Radisson Diamond," and "Seven Seas Navigator"), (3) *testimonial* ("accolades from the world's most discerning travelers"), and (4) *card stacking* (weasel word: "spacious stateroom, *most* with private balconies"). Note also the picture (the "Old World" metaphor stressing tradition), the many emotional appeals ("Sorrento red must be appreciated by all the senses," "dance through a garden of Monet's colors," "bask in the golden light of Tuscany," "enchant your ears with the spirited music of Barcelona," "savor the world with us"), and the use of "stroking," or complimenting, to flatter the reader ("tourists see the world, travelers experience it," "your thirst for the less common," "the world's most discerning travelers," "we invite you, the connoisseur").

3 Presidential inaugural addresses, from George Washington's to George W. Bush's, can help students recognize the persuasion techniques in McClintock's article. Instructors might have groups of students look at the same address and compare their findings or look at addresses in different historical periods (the language might vary, but the techniques are usually the same).

Writing Follow-up (page 169)

As an alternative to designing a magazine advertisement, students who choose Question 2 can create a television commercial and act it out in front of the class, or actually film it and show it to their classmates.

MAKING CONNECTIONS (page 170)

1 Gelernter doesn't believe in the revolutionary nature of the Internet: "We are *not* in an information age, and computers and the Internet are not a revolutionary development in human history" (par. 2). He disagrees with the writer mentioned in paragraph 10 who maintains that the Internet is "the greatest and most significant achievement in the history of mankind." In paragraph 12, Gelernter does concede that computers and the Internet have created a revolution in science and engineering but that the revolution is largely "latent, waiting to happen." Leonard, on the other hand, recognizes the revolutionary nature of the Internet: "If we accept that the creation of the globe-spanning Internet is one of the most important technological innovations of the last half of this century . . ." (par. 5). Throughout the article, he stresses the ways e-mail has profoundly changed the manner in which people interact with each other.

2 Gelernter means that new technologies create social structures that fully replace the old ones. Leonard means that e-mail blurs all social, geographical, and temporal boundaries: public/private, work/play, supervisor/employee, and so on. Despite their focus on different topics, both authors are making a similar point – that the Internet and other new technologies totally change old social structures and types of personal interaction and substitute new structures. We live in a "permanent present" with the new social patterns.

3 Through the use of personal experience, both authors are making the point that new technologies have advantages and disadvantages. Technological change is a Devil's, or Faustian, bargain, in which people gain and lose something at the same time. Depending on the perspective, technology may be a blessing or a curse.

4 McClintock doesn't mention the Internet in her article, which was written in the mid-1990s. Given her discussion, however, in paragraph 1 of the seductive nature of advertising and the mass media, people's increasing use of the Internet, the increasing incidence of spam and other types of advertising on the Internet, and people's reluctance to do the hard work of detecting and understanding the nature of propaganda (pars. 1, 23), McClintock would likely view the Internet as a great hazard to preserving "independence of thought and action" (par. 24). At the same time, however, she might argue that the Internet provides a potential tool to develop the critical thinking necessary to combat propaganda (par. 23).

5 Gelernter portrays computer games as an enjoyable, "mindless activity." Leonard describes the potential of e-mail to encourage "meaningless irrelevance," "pop-cultural triviality," and acting before thinking. McClintock depicts people as being "seduced" by the "alluring images" of advertising in the mass media (par. 1) and being willing victims of this seduction (pars. 1, 23). All three authors refer directly or indirectly to the seductive

nature of new technology; to the mindless, impulsive ways in which people interact with technology; and to people's laziness or reluctance to do the hard work of developing critical thinking skills. All three of these aspects of human nature and technology make people susceptible to the negative influence of propaganda.

ADDITIONAL READING 1 (pages 171–175)
Students Shall Not Download. Yeah, Sure. Kate Zernike

Although this article deals with college students' lax attitudes toward downloading music off the Internet, it raises the larger issue of computer ethics, often referred to as information technology ethics – the proper use of a wide range of telecommunication and data storage devices. In addition to raising questions about the ethics of music downloading, this article can be used to spark debate about the ethical nature of other computer-related behaviors: using uncited material in a paper (and whether this constitutes plagiarism); hacking into a government agency's computer system; spreading a virus; reading a friend's e-mail without permission; using e-mail and the Web for personal purposes while on the job; copying a company's software programs for personal use; and copying CDs, DVDs, and computer games. What is a harmless activity or prank for one person may be considered unethical behavior by another. The notion that the Internet has transcended ethical, moral, and legal boundaries is an important topic for students to explore.

After You Read (page 174)

For students choosing Question 1: Zernike makes her main point about plagiarism and the downloading of copyrighted material in paragraph 13 when she states, "The ease of going online has shaped not only attitudes about downloading, but cheating as well, blurring the lines between right and wrong so much that many colleges now require orientation courses. . . ." For a generation raised on the Internet where everything seems free (pars. 8, 14), downloading music does not feel inappropriate or unethical.

ADDITIONAL READING 2 (pages 176–178)
Don't Touch That Dial Madeline Drexler

In this controversial article, Drexler presents the research of Daniel Anderson, a university psychologist, who argues against the common belief that television is inherently dangerous to children. In the first half of the article, Drexler outlines Anderson's refutation of the conventional criticisms of TV and his belief that, by blaming TV for problems it doesn't cause, parents neglect their own role in helping their children grow in healthy ways. Anderson, however, doesn't argue that TV is free of negative influences: "I feel television is almost surely having a major social impact on the kids, as opposed to a cognitive impact" (par. 9). In the second half of the article, Drexler presents Anderson's beliefs about the social influence of TV and his recommendations for parents.

For a different point of view, instructors might refer students to the Web site, "Kill Your Television" <http://www.turnoffyourtv.com>, which has many links to articles discussing the negative effects of TV.

After You Read (page 178)

For students choosing Question 2: In paragraph 1, Drexler uses a simile to introduce the point Daniel Anderson will be refuting throughout the article, "Television acts as a narcotic on children – mesmerizing them, stunting their ability to think. . . ." In paragraph 13, Drexler uses the following metaphor to stress the point that TV isn't inherently positive or negative: ". . . television can be a source of enlightenment or a descent into mindlessness. . . ."

ADDITIONAL READING 3 (pages 179–181)
Conceptual Fruit Thaisa Frank

In this short story, a father, having recently discovered the Internet, tries to convey his excitement to his wife and children, only to have them dismiss his interest in various ways. A mentally handicapped daughter is the one who, in the end, teaches her father a lesson about the vacuousness of virtual reality.

Students usually enjoy this short, relatively simple story and are engaged by the questions it raises about the benefits of the Internet. When discussing the story, instructors might refer students back to the first two core readings in the chapter and ask them to consider how the narrative relates to points that Gelernter and Leonard make. Special reference might be made to paragraphs 10–12 in the first core reading, in which Gelernter describes the "cheerleading" associated with computers and the Internet and the unreal revolutions that are "locked up in awe-inspiring icebergs that just float around eliciting admiration and making trouble."

After You Read (page 181)

For students choosing Question 1: The message that Frank wishes to convey is that the Internet may, at first, appear exciting and full of possibility, but the virtual reality that it provides is never as real and useful as reality. (See especially pars. 39, 42.) Frank is poking fun at the excitement and sense of awe that new users of the Internet often experience.

For students choosing Question 2: Frank uses the metaphor of a statue ("carved from a single stone" like the work of a classical master) to emphasize the beauty and naturalness of Greta in contrast to the unreal quality of computers and the Internet.

ADDITIONAL READING 4 (page 182)

All Watched Over by Machines of Loving Grace Richard Brautigan

After You Read (page 183)

For students choosing Question 1: Brautigan portrays a vision of an ideal world in which people, technology, and nature exist in harmony. Part of the "back to nature" movement, Brautigan presents a utopian vision of a world in which computers and other forms of technology do not control people but free them to enjoy the essentials of life. His sense of urgency, however, implies that Brautigan sees a serious threat in increasing technology. The last two lines "and all watched over/by machines of loving grace" are perhaps meant to be taken ironically. The poem may be seen as an elegy – a lament on a lost pretechnological world of innocence and connection with nature.

For students choosing Question 2: The two similes in the poem are "like pure water/touching clear sky" (lines 7–8) and "where deer stroll peacefully/past computers/as if they were flowers/with spinning blossoms" (lines 13–16). Metaphors include "cybernetic meadow/where mammals and computers/live together in mutually programming harmony" (lines 3–6), "cybernetic forest/filled with pines and electronics" (lines 11–12), "our mammal/brothers and sisters" (lines 22–23), and "all watched over/by machines of loving grace" (lines 24–25).

ADDITIONAL READING 5 Humor

E-mail Mix-up (page 183)

After reading the joke, students may refer back to paragraph 13 of "We've Got Mail – Always" (page 152), where Leonard mentions one of the dangers of e-mail: messages reaching someone other than the intended audience. Students might discuss whether they have ever had this experience themselves, either sending or receiving e-mail.

Cathy Cartoon Cathy Guisewite (page 184)

This cartoon usually leads to a discussion of blogs (Web logs). Have students read or written one themselves, and what have they seen as the pros and cons of electronic journals?

Gender Roles

The theme of this chapter is gender roles, which are the culturally defined expectations and assumptions associated with female and male character and behavior. The readings and activities explore such issues as the biological and cultural origins of gender roles, negative consequences of gender stereotyping, differences in the ways females and males use language, and the role of women in the military.

The writing technique in the chapter deals with summarizing and paraphrasing – skills that students will be required to use frequently in their college studies. Students practice paraphrasing sentences and summarizing individual paragraphs and whole essays. Paraphrasing and summarizing are more difficult than they might initially seem and present a challenge even for advanced students.

CORE READING 1 (pages 189–195)

Sex Roles Hamilton McCubbin and Barbara Blum Dahl

In this textbook excerpt, the authors explore the biological, cultural, and social origins of sex roles. Most sociologists now refer to these as gender roles. Their aim is to outline the major issues in the age-old debate about the influences of nature and nurture. The authors present the existing evidence on both sides and conclude that "while the biological basis for sex-related distinctions is important, the role that society and culture play is probably more significant."

Instructors may wish to use this excerpt as an example of MLA documentation style. For an example of APA source documentation style, see "Multiple Intelligences and Emotional Intelligence" on pages 76–82 of the Student's Book.

Main Ideas (page 195)

1 A sex role refers to "the patterns of feeling and behavior deemed appropriate or inappropriate" for a female or male (par. 1). Gender identity refers to a person's concept of self as a male or female (par. 2). This identity is often shaped by the internalization of "traditional sex-role assumptions" (par. 2).

2 The authors stress that research into hormonal effects on the emotional development and behavior of females and males is in its early stages. While

such research does suggest a biological basis for gender differences, social and cultural factors are likely more important (par. 18).

3 In their chapter "Sex Roles," Hamilton McCubbin and Barbara Blum Dahl focus on the biological, cultural, and social origins of sex roles. They address the question of whether traditional sex roles are the product of nature, nurture, or some combination of the two.

Reflecting on Content (page 196)

1 Despite the authors' contention that research into hormonal influences on the formation of gender roles is at "an early and primitive stage" (par. 16) and that cultural and social influences are likely more important than biological ones (par. 18), students often find the biological evidence for the formation of gender roles persuasive. This is especially true for students from cultures where traditional gender roles are still quite strong.

2 Students from cultures with conventional gender roles tend to think that biological and anthropological factors are most important in determining gender expectations. Students from cultures with less traditional gender roles usually see cultural and social influences as more important than biological ones.

3 The word *feminism* has negative connotations for many students today. Many think of radical women concerned only with female rights and interests. It may be helpful for teachers to remind students that the meaning of the word for most social activists is more inclusive, embracing the political, economic, and social equality of the sexes.

A Writer's Technique: *Summarizing and Paraphrasing* (pages 196–197)

Summarizing (page 196)

When summarizing, students should be encouraged to use their own words and not simply copy words and phrases from the original. They should also avoid their own opinions, interpretations, and evaluations and only include the author's ideas.

1 a. When analyzing sex roles, psychologists focus on personality traits while sociologists focus on social behavior.

   b. Although biological variations exist between the sexes, culture largely determines the degree to which the differences influence gender roles.

   c. According to anthropologists, different degrees of power are associated with female and male roles.

   d. Research has shown that young children are socialized in different ways: Parents tend to indulge and support their daughters, without stressing personal achievement, whereas the same parents put pressure on their sons to accept the traditional male values of accomplishment and self-reliance.

Paraphrasing (page 197)

When paraphrasing, students should be encouraged to look for synonyms of words and phrases in the original sentence and to vary the word order and other grammatical elements. Some students like to paraphrase by reading the original sentence several times and then, without looking at it, restate the general meaning. Others prefer to go through the sentence word by word, substituting a synonym wherever possible and changing the word order.

2 a. Researchers have theorized that hormones cause some of the differences in the ways females and males behave.

b. Although biology causes differences in female and male behavior, society ultimately determines the ways in which these differences are expressed.

c. Anthropologists have pointed out that female and male roles enjoy different degrees of social power.

d. Most parents are proud of a son who excels in athletics but horrified if he expresses an interest in dancing. A more explicit paraphrase might read: Most parents are happy if a son is talented in athletics but disconcerted if he expresses an interest in the "feminine" pursuit of dancing.

Vocabulary: *Affixes and Word Roots* (pages 197–198)

This activity is very difficult for students, but work on affixes and word roots can help students figure out the meaning of unknown words from the context, without using a dictionary.

1 *inclination* consists of a prefix, a root, and a suffix: *in- + clinare + -tion.* *In-* (from Latin) means "toward." *Clinare* (from Latin) means "to lean." *-Ion* (from Latin) means an "act" or "process." *Inclination* means the act of leaning toward something (a tendency to do something).

2 *prohibit* consists of a prefix and a root: *pro- + habēre. Pro-* (from Latin and Greek) means "forward" or "in front of." *Habēre* (from Latin) means "to hold." *Prohibit* means to hold in front of something (to prevent someone from doing something).

3 *prenatal* consists of a prefix, a root, and a suffix: *pre- + natus + -al. Pre-* (from Latin) means "before." *Natus* (from Latin) means "birth." *-Al* (from Latin) means "relating to" or "characterized by." *Prenatal* means relating to a time before birth.

4 *androgen* consists of a prefix and a root: *andro-* (or *andr-*) *+ gen. Andro-* (from Greek) means "man" or "male." *Gen* (from Greek) means "producer." *Androgen* means "producer of man" (a sex hormone that produces male characteristics).

5 *sensitivity* consists of a root and a suffix: *sensatus* + *-ty*. *Sensatus* (from Latin) means "sensory." *-Ty* indicates a quality or state. *Sensitivity* means the quality or state of being sensory or sensitive, or receptive to sense impressions (an awareness of the emotions and needs of others).

6 *anthropologist* consists of a prefix, a root, and a suffix: *anthrop(o)-* + *logia* + *-ist*. *Anthrop-*, or *anthropo-* (from Latin and Greek) means a "human being." *Logia* (from Latin and Greek) means "study" or "science." *-Ist* (from Latin and Greek) means "one who specializes in something." *Anthropologist* means one who specializes in the study of human beings.

7 *complacent* consists of a prefix, a root, and a suffix: *com* + *placēre* + *-ent*. *Com-* (from Latin) means "with" or "together." *Placēre* (from Latin) means "to please." *-Ent* changes the verb *placēre* into an adjective. *Complacent* means acting with pleasure (with self-satisfaction or unconcern).

8 *dysfunctional* consists of a prefix, a root, and a suffix: *dys-* + *function* + *-al*. *Dys-* (from Latin and Greek) means "abnormal" or "impaired." *Function* (from Latin) means "performance" or "activity." *-Al* (from Latin) means "relating to" or "characterized by." *Dysfunctional* means "characterized by impaired or abnormal functioning or performance."

Discussion   (page 199)

1 Words that students often place in the female column include *domestic, gentle, patient, beautiful, obedient, passive, kind, sexy, talkative, jealous, romantic,* and *moody*. Words often placed in the male column include *active, powerful, rich, clever, ambitious, independent, brave, intelligent, aggressive,* and *competitive*. Several of these words appear in the related activity, *Vocabulary: Related Sets of Words*, on page 208.

2 The American Indian College Fund advertisement on page 220 reflects strong, positive images of women similar to those discussed in the essay "Women Have What It Takes" (pages 219–222). These images contrast with the more passive, stereotypical portrayals of women mentioned in paragraphs 1 and 26 of "Sex Roles." The Charles Atlas ad on page 224 reflects many of the male stereotypes mentioned in paragraphs 1 and 26 of "Sex Roles" and throughout the article "Boys Will Be Boys" (pages 201–206).

3 In the event that the Web site listed in this activity has changed since publication of the book, the title of the article that challenges Margaret Mead's findings is "The Science of Sex: Glenn Wilson on the Theory of Cultural Determinism." In this piece, Wilson questions Mead's conclusions about the cultural determination of gender roles, maintaining that much of her research was flawed and that the gender patterns seen in the West "are consistent with sex differences displayed by the vast majority of other species and societies."

Writing Follow-up (page 199)

Students choosing Question 3 should refer to pages 214–215 in the Student's Book for a review of summarizing.

CORE READING 2 (pages 201–206)

Boys Will Be Boys Barbara Kantrowitz and Claudia Kalb

In this article, the authors focus on differences in the emotional and social development of boys and girls, maintaining that, while girls have become freer in the expression of gender roles as a result of the feminist movement, boys, lacking such a liberation movement, have become increasingly restricted by traditional male expectations. Exploring the emotional and behavioral consequences of masculine stereotypes, the authors provide advice to parents on helping their sons deal with the challenges of male roles.

Instructors may wish to pair this article with "The Androgynous Male" (pages 223–226), a personal essay in which the author discusses the benefits males experience when freed from conventional masculine roles.

Reading Journal (page 206)

Students choosing Question 2 may be directed to page 215 in the Student's Book for a one-paragraph summary of the article.

Main Ideas (pages 206–207)

1 According to the authors, while the feminist movement has expanded the roles of girls, there has been no such liberation movement for boys (par. 11).

2 Over the last few decades, the study of child development has focused on girls. Recently, however, researchers have directed their attention to the emotional and social development of boys and the problems associated with traditional male roles. The authors' purpose is to make their audience – parents – aware of this recent research, to stress that boys are in a "silent crisis," and to provide advice on raising boys in a positive, healthy manner. Concerns of the primary parental audience are addressed in paragraphs 9, 14–17, 19–21.

3 In their article "Boys Will Be Boys," Kantrowitz and Kalb state that boys and girls have unique stages of emotional and social development, with various crisis points, and that they should be raised with their distinct needs in mind. While girls have become freer in terms of gender roles, boys have become increasingly limited by traditional masculine stereotypes, and it is thus essential for parents to help their sons break out of conventional molds and channel their innate energy into positive activities.

1 The point that the authors are making with the title is that there are certain innate male traits (e.g., physical energy and aggressiveness) and that these characteristics should not be seen as unhealthy and in need of change but as natural. Other possible titles for the article might be "The Silent Crisis of Boys" or "Raising Healthy Sons."

2 In paragraph 6, the authors maintain that "while girls' horizons have been expanding, boys' have narrowed, confined to rigid ideas of acceptable male behavior." While some students agree with this statement, others argue that girls are equally, or more limited, by gender expectations. The issue of emotional versus social opportunities and restrictions often comes up in this discussion.

3 The authors contend that "an abundance of physical energy and the urge to conquer . . . are normal male characteristics" (par. 4). This innate physicality and aggression might account for the problems boys experience in the 4–6 and 14–16 year ranges. Also contributing to the problems in these age ranges might be the traditional masculine roles boys are exposed to in the mass media: "warrior, rogue, adventurer – with heavy doses of violence" (par. 11). The authors suggest that the innate "calmness" of girls and higher proportion of nerve cells to process information contribute to the learning behaviors seen in the 0–3, 4–6, and 7–10 year ranges. The great stress on thinness and physical attractiveness in females likely contributes to anorexia, bulimia, and other eating disorders seen in the 14–16 year range.

A Writer's Technique: *Summarizing and Paraphrasing* (page 207)

Summarizing (page 207)

1 a. Although the feminist movement has led to the physicality of boys being seen as unhealthy, it should be viewed as a natural male trait that needs to be appreciated and not changed.

   b. A natural part of growing up is the tug between emotional closeness with, and independence from, one's parents, but some researchers think the process of parental separation has become overly abrupt, resulting in the repression of love and other essential emotions.

   c. Masculine stereotypes in the mass media involving aggression, toughness, and violence encourage boys to repress positive, nurturing emotions and to behave in angry, forceful ways.

   d. Because boys tend to lose emotional and verbal contact with their parents as they get older, it is essential for parents to try to break through the barriers and communicate with their sons as much as possible.

Paraphrasing (page 207)

2 a. As a result of the feminist movement, even typical behavior of boys is regarded as unhealthy.

   b. The conventional way of looking at the development of boys and girls through a single lens had serious weaknesses.

   c. Although girls have become freer in terms of gender roles, boys have continued to be limited by traditional masculine stereotypes.

   d. Research into biological influences on human development is still in its infancy.

   e. The onset of the teenage years turns what once was the emotional warmth of young boys into sullen distance and total lack of communication with parents.

Vocabulary: *Related Sets of Words*   (page 208)

This activity often results in a spirited debate about female and male personality traits, especially the placement of the words *aggressive, competitive, jealous, obstinate,* and *sophisticated*. Students should be encouraged to consider the expression of traits in different contexts – formal versus informal, personal versus social, small- versus large-group interaction, and so on. Other words that might be added to the list include *talkative, dogmatic, sensual, reliable, charismatic, nurturing, intelligent, seductive, creative, chaste, patient, cruel,* and *vain*.

Discussion   (page 209)

1 Inappropriate behaviors that students often place in the female column include those involving aggression, toughness, competition, ambition, and sex (e.g., premarital sex and promiscuity). Inappropriate male behaviors often include crying and other public displays of emotion, as well as actions reflecting vulnerability, tenderness, compassion, sensitivity, and effeminateness. It is not surprising that the behaviors considered inappropriate for females are seen as appropriate for males, and vice versa.

2 Students often enjoy this hands-on, community activity, where they observe gender images and stereotypes. As a related activity, students might go to an art museum and examine representations of females and males in terms of images, roles, values, ideals, and social messages.

3 In this short, humorous Web broadcast, a stay-at-home Dad discusses traditional and changing gender roles. The man's embracing of nontraditional male roles is similar to that of Noel Perrin in "The Androgynous Male" (pages 223–226).

Students choosing Question 3 should refer to pages 214–215 in the Student's Book for a review of summarizing.

CORE READING 3 (pages 211–213)

Sex, Sighs, and Conversation: Why Men and Women Can't Communicate Deborah Tannen

This short article explores "cross-cultural" differences in the ways females and males use language and the frustrations these differences cause when women and men converse. Tannen's basic contention is that females use language to make connections and foster intimacy, whereas males use language to preserve independence and negotiate status.

Students usually enjoy discussing the topic of gender variations in language use and often relate personal experiences that support or contradict Tannen's findings. Most students tend to agree with Tannen's thesis but feel that, due to changing gender roles, the language distinctions she mentions are not as strong as in the past and are reflective of an older generation.

Main Ideas (page 214)

1 According to Tannen, females use language to "negotiate intimacy" (par. 3). Language helps women share feelings, make connections, and create a sense of closeness and harmony. In contrast, males tend to use language to "preserve independence and negotiate their status" (par. 4). Language helps men remain the center of attention, challenge and compete with others, and demonstrate knowledge and verbal agility.

2 Tannen means that, although people like to see themselves as unique individuals, they are always a product of their culture. In order to avoid misunderstandings, conflicts, and other problems, men and women need to be aware of gender differences in language use.

3 In her article "Sex, Sighs, and Conversation," Deborah Tannen maintains that there are gender differences in the use of language and that this often leads to frustration when women and men converse. In order to minimize conflict and improve relationships, men and women need to be aware of these "cross-cultural" differences in language use.

Reflecting on Content (page 214)

1 The use of language by girls and women reflects traditional female roles and expectations: making connections with people, providing emotional support, creating intimacy and harmony, and expressing feelings openly. The use of language by boys and men reflects traditional male roles and expectations

such as establishing independence, competing with others, offering advice, and hiding emotions.

2 The primary audience for the article is people in opposite-sex relationships. In order to support her points about gender differences in language, Tannen provides many examples relating to boyfriends and girlfriends and husbands and wives. In the last two paragraphs, Tannen discusses the need for partners to be aware of gender differences in language use and to make adjustments in order to improve their relationships.

3 By "cross-cultural," Tannen means that females and males grow up in very different ways in distinct "cultures." They are socialized to different roles, behaviors, and values.

A Writer's Technique: *Summarizing and Paraphrasing* (pages 214–215)

Summarizing (pages 214–215)

1 In her article "Sex, Sighs, and Conversation: Why Men and Women Can't Communicate," Deborah Tannen focuses on gender differences in the use of language and on the frustration these differences cause when women and men converse. She starts with an anecdote about a woman and a man who are lost. The woman wants to ask for directions and the man doesn't. Tannen then outlines the major differences in the ways females and males use language. Beginning in early childhood, girls learn to use language to share feelings with their female friends and to create a sense of closeness. Boys, on the other hand, learn to use language to establish their independence and compete with their male friends. Tannen goes on to give a number of examples of the ways in which these different expectations about the functions of language continue into adulthood and cause problems. Her examples involve conversations such as the one in the opening anecdote and the ways in which women use language to create intimacy and harmony and men to enhance their status and challenge others. Tannen concludes her article by stressing the need for female and male partners to recognize that they often converse in different ways. If women and men become aware of these "cross-cultural" differences, they will stop assuming that their own ways of speaking are correct and that those of their partners are wrong, and they will make the small changes necessary to improve communication.

Paraphrasing (pages 215–216)

2 a. Different expectations about the functions of language continue into adulthood and cause frustration or confusion when men and women converse.

   b. When men provide advice, they place themselves in a higher position than women, which creates a sense of distance contrary to what the women intended in starting the conversation.

c. There are many ways that men challenge the position of others instead of offering support as women do.

d. Being aware that a partner's actions are a normal reflection of gender and not the person's own fault can reduce conflict in relationships.

Vocabulary: *Connotations of Words*   (page 216)

This exercise helps students understand the distinction between denotations and connotations of words and raises questions about gender roles, stereotypes, and double standards.

- *lady/gentleman:* Both words are courteous references. To some people, *lady* is a negative term, connoting a dainty, conventional, often docile woman.

- *widow/widower:* Both words refer to people whose spouse has died and who have not remarried. In English, when the meaning relates to marriage, domesticity, or traditional female professions, the base term is usually the female term with a male variation – e.g., *widow, housewife, nurse,* and *bride.* In contrast, when the meaning relates to traditional male professions and positions, the male term tends to be the base, with a female variation, as in *fireman, policeman, chairman, landlord,* and *businessman.*

- Miss/Mr.: *Miss* refers to an unmarried woman or girl, whereas *Mr.* is a neutral reference to a man who is married or unmarried. Note the difference between *Miss, Mrs.,* and *Ms.* suggesting the traditional importance of marriage in women's lives.

- *mistress/master:* Both words refer to people in positions of power, authority, or ownership. (An additional meaning of *mistress* is a woman other than his wife with whom a married man is having a continuing sexual relationship.)

- *spinster/bachelor:* Both words refer to unmarried people. *Spinster,* a word with somewhat negative connotations, refers to an unmarried woman past the common age for marrying, whereas *bachelor* is a more neutral term referring to an unmarried man of any age.

- *tomboy/sissy:* Both words refer to people behaving in a manner considered more common or appropriate for the opposite sex. Note the negative connotations of *sissy* – an effeminate male or a timid, cowardly person.

- *housewife/househusband* (or *stay-at-home dad*): Both words refer to married people in charge of the household while their partner earns the family income.

- *hostess/host:* Both words refer to people who entertain socially. The suffix *-ess* indicates a female, as in *waitress, actress,* and *stewardess,* which is often considered sexist.

- *nurse/male nurse:* Both words refer to people trained to care for the sick or infirm.

- *landlady/landlord:* Both words refer to owners of property that is rented to another.

- *bride/groom:* Both words refer to people just married or about to be married. The term *bridegroom* is a male equivalent of the female base term *bride.*

- *chairwoman/chairman:* Both words refer to a presiding officer of a meeting, organization, or committee. *Chair* and *chairperson* are increasingly used to refer to both sexes.

- *maid/butler:* Both words refer to household servants. A maid does domestic work, whereas a butler may be in charge of other household employees. A second meaning of *maid* – a young unmarried female – does not have a male counterpart.

- *witch/wizard* (or *sorcerer*): Both words refer to people with magical powers. A witch is usually associated with evil, whereas a wizard is someone skilled in magic. A witch may also refer to an ugly old woman or hag, but there is no similar term for men.

- *stewardess/steward:* Both words refer to employees who attend passengers on a ship, airplane, or train. *Flight attendant* is now commonly used for both sexes working in airplanes.

- *businesswoman/businessman:* Both words refer to people who transact business. *Business executive* or *businessperson* is now commonly used for both sexes.

Discussion   (page 217)

1 Most students agree in general with Tannen's comments about gender differences in language use, but feel that things are changing somewhat today, with males being encouraged to express their emotions more and females to assert themselves more. Students might refer to the second core reading, "Boys Will Be Boys," in which the authors argue that boys are as emotionally unexpressive as ever.

2 For a discussion of the ways in which gender differences in language use are reflected in the classroom, see Deborah Tannen's article "Teachers' Classroom Strategies Should Recognize That Men and Women Use Language Differently" from *The Chronicle of Higher Education*, June 19, 1991. In this piece, Tannen argues that speaking in a classroom "is more congenial to boys' language experience than to girls', since it entails putting oneself forward in front of a large group of people . . . [often in a] debate-like format." She also discusses the use of small groups to encourage female students to participate more.

3 Tannen's home page <www.georgetown.edu/faculty/tannend/> has several links to written interviews, chat groups, and radio interviews. When linking to other sites, students may need to perform a search for "Deborah Tannen," using quotation marks to locate the interviews within that Web site.

Writing Follow-up (page 217)

Students choosing Question 3 should refer to pages 214–215 in the Student's Book for a review of summarizing.

MAKING CONNECTIONS (page 218)

1 Michael Gurian and the authors of "Sex Roles" would certainly agree that biological factors are important in shaping gender roles. In paragraph 4 of "Boys Will Be Boys," Gurian speaks of "normal male characteristics" and says that "boys will be boys" and we shouldn't try to "rewire" them. In paragraph 6, he mentions boys who use dolls as guns, implying a strong biological element. Like the authors of the first article, however, he believes that social factors are essential in determining gender roles. Also in paragraph 6, he speaks of an awareness of "the biological realities and the sociological realities" of gender roles.

2 The gender differences in language use that Tannen discusses might be explained by biological, anthropological, or social factors. In paragraphs 12–13 of "Sex Roles," the authors mention hormonal differences that seem to be related to male aggression and female nurturance. In paragraph 21, they mention anthropological distinctions between gender roles, where power and prestige are associated with men and domestic activities with women. And in paragraph 27, the authors discuss the socialization of boys to value achievement and independence, whereas the same values are not stressed in girls' development.

3 The researchers mentioned in "Boys Will Be Boys" might disagree with part of point four of the feminist power analysis of gender roles. Although they would agree with the first half of the contention – that men are oppressed because of traditional male roles that deemphasize emotional expression and nurturance – they might disagree with the second half, maintaining that men are oppressed, in certain ways, as women are, *because* of their sex. The researchers might argue that, due to the male macho stereotypes mentioned in paragraph 11, women have been favored over men in "nurturing" professions and roles such as elementary school teachers, nurses, obstetricians, and stay-at-home parents.

4 Tannen would probably say that the linguistic behaviors of the boys mentioned in "Boys Will Be Boys" – gunplay as a greeting (par. 1) and noncommunication (pars. 15–16) – are language patterns that boys learn at a very young age. These patterns reflect the values of independence, status, and emotional restraint.

5 Kantrowitz and Kalb suggest that boys need to change in some ways – not in terms of their biological male traits but in terms of the macho ideal that limits emotional expression (pars. 10–11) and leads to homophobia (par. 13),

antisocial behavior (see chart, page 202), and, in extreme cases, suicide (par. 15). Similarly, Tannen stresses the need for females and males to "make small adjustments [in their behavior and speech] that will please their partners and improve the relationship" (par. 16).

ADDITIONAL READING 1 (pages 219–222)
Women Have What It Takes Carol Barkalow

In this short personal essay, Barkalow, an army officer, argues that women should be allowed to engage in frontline military combat if they so choose. Reviewing some of the traditional attitudes toward women and the military, she maintains that if women have the same training as men, and are as physically and mentally capable, they should be allowed to serve in all types of combat units.

This essay and the accompanying letter to the editor, "An Opposing View" by Bill Norton, which argues against women serving in combat units, usually stimulate vocal debate among students. Instructors might have students read the piece at home or in class, write a brief reaction, and then debate the issue either in small groups or as a class.

Barkalow's essay may be paired with the following reading, "The Androgynous Male," as examples of a woman and a man arguing the need to break out of conventional gender roles and engage in activities traditionally associated with the opposite sex.

Before You Read (page 219)

See the comments for Question 2 in *Discussion* on page 49 of this manual.

ADDITIONAL READING 2 (pages 223–226)
The Androgynous Male Noel Perrin

Near the beginning of this personal essay, Perrin states that there are a large number of women and men who are androgynous and that this frees them from the restrictions of traditional gender roles. He then goes on to discuss what it means to be "spiritually androgynous" (par. 7) and the freedom he has personally experienced from not having to fulfill the "single ideal of the dominant male" (par. 10).

This essay often leads to debate about the advantages and disadvantages of being female or male, "appropriate" and "inappropriate" female and male behavior, and traditional versus changing gender roles. The piece may be paired with the previous reading, "Women Have What It Takes," as examples of arguments in favor of less rigid gender roles, or with the second core reading, "Boys Will Be Boys," which discusses the conventional masculine expectations that Perrin sees as limiting.

Before You Read (page 223)

See Question 2 in *Discussion* for the first core reading "Sex Roles," on page 49 of this manual.

ADDITIONAL READING 3 (pages 227–232)
The Princess and the Admiral Charlotte Pomerantz

As stated in the headnote to the story, this fable is based on the thirteenth-century invasion of Vietnam by Kublai Kahn and his Imperial Navy. This Mongol emperor, known for his fierce military forces, defeated the Sung dynasty of China in 1279, but his campaigns against Japan, Indonesia, and other Southeast Asian countries ended in failure. In this "upside-down" fairytale, where traditional female roles are reversed, a young princess outwits a powerful admiral and his fleet, ensuring the continuation of a century of peace in her small kingdom.

This story often leads to vocal debate about the virtues of male versus female leaders of countries. Given the differences in female and male character, behavior, and communication style that Deborah Tannen discusses in the third core reading, some would contend that men are naturally better at leading people and making important national and international decisions. Others would argue that females are better suited intellectually and emotionally to being leaders and that they do a better job of creating a humane and peaceful world.

Before You Read (page 227)

Regarding the bar graph, most of the female heads of state in Europe have been from the northern part of the continent, including Norway, Finland, Iceland, Denmark, the United Kingdom, and the Netherlands. Most of the female heads of state in Asia have been from the Indian subcontinent, including India, Bangladesh, and Pakistan.

After You Read (page 233)

For students choosing Question 2: There are striking differences between the Princess and the Admiral in terms of leadership styles, military strategies, and ways of interacting and speaking with people. The Princess is associated with peace (pars. 4, 70, 75, 96–97); reflection, deliberation, patience (pars. 22–26); feeling and intuition (pars. 4, 31, 97); and openness to alternatives (par. 28). The Princess demonstrates the forces of nature versus human weaponry (pars. 26, 44); decisiveness (par. 35); resourcefulness (pars. 26, 50); and intelligence and cleverness versus physical force (pars. 26, 44). She shows mercy, kindness, gentleness, concern (pars. 84, 88, 89, 92); and equality of the sexes (pars. 37, 90). In contrast, the Admiral is associated with giving commands (pars. 47, 60, 62), self-satisfaction and arrogance (pars. 51, 53, 54, 56, 67), intimidation (par. 53), and physical force and violence (pars. 47, 54). The admiral desmonstrates plunder (par. 54); sexism (pars. 56, 80, 90); loud, assertive language (pars. 58, 60, 74); and insulting and mocking language (pars. 56, 64). He shows impatience and anger (pars. 62, 74) and defiance and stubbornness (pars. 72, 76). At the end, the Admiral has learned a powerful lesson about gender stereotyping and expresses emotion and gratitude (traditional female traits).

ADDITIONAL READING 4 (pages 233–234)
The Greater God Rakesh Ratti

In this poem, an Indian American author contrasts the negative ways in which he saw his mother as a child (a fearful, powerless female servant) with the positive ways he came to see her at an older age (a strong, kind, loving god). This poem can lead to discussions of traditional versus changing gender roles, sexual discrimination, relationships between children and their parents, and mythological associations of women and divinity.

In order to reflect more on gender roles, students might write a poem of their own dealing with their relationships to, and perceptions of, their mother or father.

After You Read (page 234)

For students choosing Question 1: The positive female roles and expectations reflected in the poem include divinity (lines 1, 19, 35); gentleness, kindness, love (lines 13, 15, 31); respect for others (lines 17–18); center of the family (lines 20–21); self-sacrifice (lines 9–11, 22); support and nourishment of others (lines 23–24); and discipline (line 27). Negative female roles and expectations include fear and timidity (lines 3, 16); restricted domestic life (line 8); little social power and slavish subservience to men (lines 4, 6–9, 32); silence (lines 9–10); and excessive yielding (line 14).

ADDITIONAL READING 5 Humor
The Gender of Computers (page 235)

This joke usually leads to a discussion of gender roles and stereotypes, as well as the use of masculine and feminine pronouns in different languages. In English, the feminine pronoun is frequently used for countries, machines, ships, cars, and other vehicles to suggest a feeling of fondness for, or familiarity with, an object. The feminine pronoun is also sometimes used in a figurative sense for things to reflect a sense of beauty, kindness, or fertility (e.g., "The sun casts *her* warmth on people's hearts" or "The earth shares *her* wealth with all those in need").

Cathy Cartoon Cathy Guisewite (page 236)

This cartoon raises interesting questions about traditional versus changing gender roles, gender-role stereotyping, and the extent to which it is possible to raise children free from gender expectations.

Work

The focus of this chapter is people's attitudes toward their work. The readings and activities explore such issues as job satisfaction, career goals, definitions of success and the American Dream, and cross-cultural differences in work values.

The writing technique in the chapter involves tone, which is an author's attitude toward his or her subject as reflected in the choice of words and details. Students practice identifying the varying tones in reading passages and write in different tones themselves.

CORE READING 1 (pages 241–245)
The New American Dreamers Ruth Sidel

In this chapter excerpt, Sidel focuses on the goals and aspirations of the "New American Dreamers" – young women in the United States who dream about controlling their own personal and professional destinies and achieving material success. After sketching the lives of several young women from different ethnic backgrounds and social classes, Sidel addresses the question of how realistic these women's chances are of actually achieving the "American Dream."

This piece often leads to discussions of success, the American Dream, students' personal and professional goals, and career opportunities for women and men.

Main Ideas (page 245)

1 The "New American Dreamers" are young women in the United States, who since the mid-1960s, have been encouraged to take control of their personal and professional lives and to pursue the same American Dream of success that men have traditionally sought (see pars. 7–8, 11, 17–18).

2 The major aspects of the American Dream that Sidel discusses are "the good life," including one's own home, professional career, material success (pars. 8, 11–12); a happy marriage with children and joint parental responsibility (pars. 4, 15); a sense of optimism, including upward social mobility (par. 11); personal choice (par. 11); and a belief that, with enough hard work and determination, one can control one's own destiny and "have it all" (pars. 1, 11, 17–18). See also the reference to the Horatio Alger rags-to-riches myth in paragraph 13.

3 In her essay "The New American Dreamers," Ruth Sidel maintains that young American women from all social classes, ethnic groups, and geographical areas have the same dream for the future: being able to control their own personal and professional destiny and achieving material success. Yet in spite of the optimistic view of American women that, with enough hard work they can accomplish whatever they want, the chances of achieving the American Dream are limited for many.

Reflecting on Content   (page 245)

1 The title contains a clever reference to the "American Dream" and focuses attention on the "new" dreamers – young American women. Other possible titles include "Having It All," "Women as Heroines of Their Own Lives," and "The Female Horatio Alger."

2 At the end of paragraph 17, Sidel implies that, due to changing social expectations about the control females have in their personal and professional lives, the chances of their achieving the New American Dream are stronger than in the past. However, despite the optimism the young women have (pars. 1, 11, 17–18), Sidel believes that the chances of success for many are very limited. This is true of those living in poverty, those with substance abuse problems, and those who are illiterate. For these people, the New American Dream is probably an "impossible dream" (pars. 13, 16). "And yet, maybe . . ." (par. 16).

3 Many students share the sense of optimism expressed by the young women in the reading and have similar hopes and dreams of personal and professional success. Depending, however, on their cultural and personal backgrounds, students vary in their degree of optimism.

A Writer's Technique: *Tone*   (pages 246–247)

Recognizing the tone of a piece of writing – an important reading skill – can be difficult even for quite advanced students. Thus instructors may wish to have students do this exercise in small groups.

1 objective 2 anxious 3 enthusiastic 4 longing 5 determined

Vocabulary: *Synonyms*   (pages 247–248)

1 antithesis 2 accurately 3 intricately 4 self-absorbed 5 respond to
6 abandoned 7 pervasive 8 mundane

Discussion   (page 249)

1 In addition to discussing the four questions relating to their career goals, students might consider whether they share the New American Dreamers'

sense of optimism. This activity often leads to discussions of career choice, training, and opportunity, especially from the perspective of gender.

2 Students might be directed to the following collections of oral histories: *American Dreams: Lost and Found,* by Studs Terkel (Ballantine, 1980); *New Americans/An Oral History: Immigrants and Refugees in the U.S. Today,* edited by Al Santoli (Viking, 1988); *The Immigrant Experience: the Anguish of Becoming American,* edited by Thomas C. Wheeler (Penguin, 1971); and *Visions of America: Personal Narratives from the Promised Land,* edited by Wesley Brown and Amy Ling (Persea, 1993).

3 Students usually enjoy taking the Jung Typology test, identifying their personality type, and seeing the careers to which they might be well suited. According to the Jung/Myers-Briggs typology, people can be classified using four criteria: Extroversion/Introversion, Sensing/Intuition, Thinking/Feeling, and Judging/Perceiving. Different combinations of these criteria determine a personality type, for example, ISTJ: Introvert/Sensing/Thinking/Judging.

Writing Follow-up   (page 249)

Students choosing Question 1: In this exercise the details of the paragraph and/or the style may be changed. Instructors might remind students that style refers to the individual manner in which a writer expresses his or her ideas. Style includes sentence structure, organization, tone, and use of figurative language.

CORE READING 2 (pages 251–255)
Someone Is Stealing Your Life Michael Ventura

In this personal essay, Ventura describes the exploitation that most U.S. workers experience throughout their lives resulting in a lack of freedom, authority, and human dignity that turns their lives into drudgery and slavery. Ventura passionately argues that workers need to take back their lives, which are being "stolen" from them, and demand a more equitable and humane work environment from their employers, where their voices and concerns are heard and their contributions are valued.

This essay usually leads to a discussion of different types of jobs (blue-collar, white-collar, professional) and the reasons some people find their jobs enjoyable and rewarding and others do not. The piece also provides an opportunity for students to examine the ways in which a writer manipulates tone to support his points. If they have not already done so, it may be valuable for students to read the notes and practice the exercise in *A Writer's Technique: Tone* on pages 246–247 of the Student's Book.

Main Ideas (page 255)

1 By "an illusion of freedom" (par. 6), Ventura means that employers try to give workers a sense of a free, humane workplace in order to keep them content but never really give them any true freedom, power, or dignity. He uses the examples of vacation, salary, health insurance, and pension to show how employers give their workers just enough to keep them "sweet" but "not enough to make life different" (par. 7).

2 According to Ventura, Americans lack power in the workplace in the following ways: They take orders like "slaves," have little or no authority over what they do, and have no say in important management decisions (pars. 2, 4, 13). Their labor, skill, and talent aren't valued monetarily (par. 11), and they have little share in company profits (pars. 7, 8, 13, 16).

3 In the article "Someone Is Stealing Your Life," Michael Ventura argues that U.S. workers are slaves who lack power, freedom, and dignity in the workplace and whose labor, skill, and talents are not valued by those in control. Workers are the lifeline of any company and need to be treated fairly and justly in terms of salary, benefits, and profit sharing, and should have a voice in important management decisions.

Reflecting on Content (page 255)

1 Ventura's purpose in writing the article is to convince his readers that U.S. workers are being exploited by those in control. He contends that they lack freedom, power, and dignity in the workplace and that they deserve a better salary, a share in company profits, and a voice in management decisions. Workers are being treated unfairly by employers and need to take back their lives by demanding a more humane workplace.

2 Most students agree with Ventura that money is the bottom line in the workplace and that workers are being exploited by those in control (see *Journal Writing* on page 250). Although students tend to agree with Ventura's basic assertion about the lack of freedom and power in the workplace, they sometimes feel that he is overstating his point. This often results in a useful discussion of a writer's tone and the most effective ways to convince a reader of something.

3 As in the previous question, these issues often lead to a discussion of the most effective ways to present arguments logically and emotionally, including the use of provocation and analogy. In paragraph 5, Ventura concedes that he is writing in a "fairly harsh way" and that he might sound "radical," but he argues that his statements about the U.S. workplace are accurate since they're based on personal experience. He uses striking analogies at the end to make his point about the oppression of workers – theft of workers' lives (pars. 14–16, 20) and the commission of a crime by employers (par. 19).

A Writer's Technique: *Tone* (page 256)

1 objective 2 sarcastic 3 self-evident 4 aggressive (determined)

Vocabulary: *Collocations* (pages 256–257)

The following collocations are the ones that appear in the reading. Alternatives are placed in parentheses. With several alternatives for some word combinations, this becomes a challenging exercise, even for advanced students.

1 f (b, d, e, h) 2 i (g) 3 j (g) 4 b (c, d, h) 5 h (b, d) 6 a (i) 7 d 8 c (b, h, i)
9 e (b, d, f, h) 10 g (a)

Discussion (page 258)

1 Regarding employees, Ventura criticizes the lack of the following in the U.S. workplace: freedom (pars. 2–4), dignity (par. 4), power (pars. 11–13, 16), profit sharing (pars. 7–8, 13, 16), say in important management decisions (pars. 2, 4, 13), and employer recognition of workers' labor, skill, and talent (par. 11). Ventura also points to poor salaries and benefits (pars. 6–7) and a drone-like existence (pars. 2–3, 5) as workplace difficulties.

2 This activity provides an opportunity for students to describe their ideal job. They might consider such aspects of employment as the type of work, degree of responsibility, level of stress, salary, length of workday, vacation, benefits, job security, and commute time.

3 Students usually enjoy this activity and find it relevant to their personal and professional lives.

Writing Follow-up (page 258)

Students choosing Question 1 will not only be engaged in the topic of work but also be made aware of the importance of tone in writing, especially persuasive writing.

For students choosing Question 3: After students have written a cover letter for a position, instructors might have them imagine that they are part of a search committee looking for the most qualified candidate. After discussing several of their classmates' letters in a small group, they can decide which candidate they would hire and why.

CORE READING 3 (pages 260–263)
Our Schedules, Our Selves Jay Walljasper

In this essay, Walljasper discusses the increasingly fast-paced life of North Americans and the negative consequences of their "dizzying timetable of duties, commitments, demands, and options" (par. 3). After arguing that the tyranny of the schedule diminishes one's ability to enjoy life's small, unexpected pleasures, Walljasper offers several suggestions to help free people from their hectic lifestyles.

Like the author of the previous article, "Someone Is Stealing Your Life," Walljasper contends that people, especially those at the bottom of the socioeconomic ladder, need greater control over their work lives, including better pay, more vacation time, and a share in company profits.

Main Ideas   (page 263)

1 The main factors contributing to people's increasingly hectic lifestyle include a "dizzying timetable of duties, commitments, demands, and options" on the job, in school, and at home (par. 3); the "daily grind" of life (par. 2); a globalized economy accompanied by decreasing control over one's salary and working conditions (par. 4); an "industrialized fast-paced society" (par. 14); demanding jobs, two-worker households, and single-parent families (par. 10); new technologies (e.g., cell phones, e-mail, laptop computers) that contribute to a fast pace of life; and the human desire for more choices and new experiences (par. 6).

2 The results of an increasingly fast-paced, schedule-driven life are that people miss out on the "joyous details of everyday life" (par. 10) and memorable, spontaneous moments that make one feel alive (pars. 8, 12); "idle moments, reflective pauses, and serendipity" (par. 2); "luxurious leisure" (par. 3); and fun (par. 7). The small joys of life that one misses out on include stopping to talk to a friend (pars. 2, 7); appreciating a sunny afternoon or a balmy spring evening (pars. 2, 8); cooking and attending block parties (par. 10); strolling around town and making popcorn in front of the fireplace (par. 12); rollerblading and playing chess (par. 13); and making love (par. 14). In addition, with too many activities and a slave-like use of technology (par. 5), people become exhausted (par. 2), and children have little time for relaxed, neighborhood play (par. 8).

3 In the essay "Our Schedules, Our Selves," Jay Walljasper argues that, due to increasingly fast-paced lifestyles filled with prescheduled activities, responsibilities, and options, North Americans have become overwhelmed by activities and miss out on life's small, unexpected pleasures. In order to be freed from the yoke of an overscheduled personal and professional life and to lead a more fulfilling existence, people need to cut back on their daily appointments, and employers need to provide a more humane workplace, including a shortened workweek and more vacation time.

Reflecting on Content   (page 264)

1 Students usually become very engaged in this topic of the pros and cons of new technologies – the Faustian, or Devil's bargain, by which people gain and

lose something at the same time (see par. 5, in which Walljasper discusses the ways in which technology both facilitates and complicates our lives). This is the same issue that Leonard explores in "We've Got Mail – Always," the second core reading in Chapter 3, page 149.

2 The suggestions that Walljasper makes to help free people from their hectic lifestyles include more vacation time; a shortened work week; sabbaticals every ten years for all workers; paid holidays; and more clout and flexibility in the workplace, including stronger unions and employee ownership (par. 11). He also recommends that people schedule fewer activities (par. 12), set aside some free time on their calendar (par. 13), and think of time not as a "mechanized instrument to be programmed" but as something that has "its own ever-shifting shape and rhythms" (par. 14). This reconception of time will help liberate people from the tyranny of schedules.

3 Teachers may wish to have students review the section "Time" (pages 10–11) in "American Values and Assumptions," the first core reading in Chapter 1, in which the author discusses cultural differences in perceptions of time. Also see "Time Talks, with an Accent," the third core reading in Chapter 1 (page 27), which similarly deals with cultural variations in concepts of time, including pace of life; rules of punctuality; and orientation to past, present, or future.

A Writer's Technique: *Tone* (pages 264–265)

Unlike the tone exercises for the first two core readings in which students choose words from a list, this activity has students think of adjectives of their own to describe the tone of passages. Since this tone activity is more difficult than the ones for the other core readings, instructors might have students work in small groups.

1 Although the adjective *relieved* reflects the tone of the last sentence ("Whew!"), *frantic* or *hectic* better describes the tone of the rest of the passage.

2 Although *relieved* reflects the tone of the first three sentences of the passage, *frustrated* better describes the tone of the last four sentences.

3 This passage reflects an *objective* tone.

4 This passage reflects an *enthusiastic* or *excited* tone.

Vocabulary: *Phrasal Verbs* (page 265)

1 blow off 2 add up to 3 holding down 4 miss out on 5 cut back 6 fell through 7 get away with 8 setting aside

Discussion (pages 266–267)

1 For the first two columns, see the comments for Questions 1 and 2 in *Main Ideas* on the opposite page. For the third column, see the comments for Question 2 in *Reflecting on Content* on the opposite page.

2 For the survey, students can think of questions relating to the three columns in the chart for *Discussion* 1: causes of stress, results of stress, and ways to deal with stress. For an online test relating to stress, with multiple questions that determine whether one has a Type A, B, or A/B personality, see the Glazer Stress Control Lifestyle Questionnaire <www.brelaxed.co.uk/page3.htm> .

3 "Vacationless by Choice" presents interviews with Americans who bury themselves in their work and say they don't need a vacation (apparently 25 percent of U.S. workers). "Do Americans Get Enough Vacation Time?" (do not use the question mark in the search) addresses the issue of whether Americans need more vacation time. "French Vacations" discusses the trend of French workers staggering their vacation times throughout the year as opposed to taking a traditional five-week vacation in August, which has caused turmoil in the hotel and resort industry.

Writing Follow-up (page 267)

Students choosing Question 1 might read their paragraphs to several classmates and see if their audience can guess the basic tone of the passages.

MAKING CONNECTIONS (page 268)

1 The women in the first reading express a great sense of optimism – a belief that, with enough hard work and determination, they can control their own destinies and achieve personal and professional success. Ventura, on the other hand, is more pessimistic and harsh in his assessment of the chances of people to achieve the American Dream. He maintains that most people have little control over their professional lives. They will not achieve the dream of life, liberty, and the pursuit of happiness, including material success, which the young women in the first reading take for granted. Ventura would agree with Sidel that, for many, this is an impossible dream.

2 Ventura maintains that Americans are slaves (par. 4) in the workplace: they take orders; have little or no authority over what they do; have no say in important management decisions; and receive too little salary, vacation, health insurance, pension, and share in company profits. Their labor, skill, and talent aren't valued; they are exploited financially; and they lack freedom, power, and dignity in their working lives. Similarly Walljasper contends that, on the job, people are "virtual slaves" (par. 3). With an increasingly globalized economy, employees, especially those at the bottom of the socioeconomic ladder, have little control over their work lives. They often

WORK 69

hold down two or three jobs, can't pay their bills, work weekends and have too little income, vacation time, and share in company profits.

3 Walljasper would probably advise the young women, as they pursue their personal and professional dreams, not to get too caught up in material success, not to try to map out their entire futures, and not to become slaves to their busy schedules. He would likely urge the women to take time to enjoy the "joyous details of everyday life" (par. 10).

4 Ventura and Walljasper both make the following suggestions to help employees feel more in control of their lives: better pay, more vacation time, profit sharing, and a greater say in decisions affecting the workplace.

5 The predominant tone of the first reading is one of realism. In the second reading the tone is anger, and in the third reading, loss. Sidel withholds personal judgment, first describing the sense of optimism that young women have in achieving personal and professional success. She goes on to describe the stark reality, the "impossible dream," that faces many of these women. The only place where Sidel's own voice is heard is in paragraph 16, where she creates a tone of longing and regret. In contrast to the largely objective tone of the first reading, the tone of Ventura's essay is highly subjective; in an assertive and harsh voice, he negatively assesses the U.S. workplace, maintaining that the American Dream is a fantasy for most workers. In the third reading, Walljasper alternates between an objective and a subjective tone. He remains objective when discussing the socioeconomic reasons for people's hectic lifestyles and becomes more subjective when dealing with the negative consequences of this fast-paced life and ways to reverse this loss and enjoy life's small pleasures. Unlike Ventura, Walljasper is more optimistic in his belief that people can take back their lives and enjoy the magic, spontaneous moments.

ADDITIONAL READING 1 (pages 269–273)

The Rage to Know Horace Freeland Judson

This chapter excerpt discusses the various reasons scientists are involved in their professions, including the pleasures, challenges, and discoveries associated with scientific endeavor. Focusing on the motivations of well-known scientists throughout history, Judson creates a vivid picture of the creative process, with all of the joys and frustrations it entails.

The pleasure, excitement, and freedom that the scientists experience contrast strongly with the dissatisfaction, stress, and powerlessness encountered by the employees in the second and third core readings in this chapter and with the exploitation and backbreaking work of the Mexican laborers in the second additional reading, "Los Pobres." The optimism of the scientists is similar to that expressed by the young women in the first core reading; however, the scientists' primary motivation is not material success but delight in making sense of the world.

For students choosing Question 1: The major motivations of the scientists include the exhilaration of experiencing "the moment of truth" about the world and the beauty revealed in these "luminous moments of discovery" (pars. 2–3), the search for unity in diversity with its "astonishing simplicities" (par. 3), and pride in one's skill (par. 4). Still other motivations are recognition by one's colleagues and ambition for fame (par. 4), competition and challenge (pars. 4, 7), fun play of the mind (par. 4), curiosity and delight in putting the world together (par. 7), the rage to know and the search for enlightenment (pars. 7–8, 10), and the freedom of inquiry (par. 11).

ADDITIONAL READING 2 (pages 274–277)

Los Pobres Richard Rodriguez

In this autobiographical excerpt, Rodriguez describes a summer construction job he had after graduating from college that led to a powerful revelation about personal and social identity. Instead of easily learning what "real work" was like, as he had expected, Rodriguez instead came face to face with the "disadvantaged condition" of *los pobres* – the vulnerability and exploitation of migrant Mexican farm workers who do hard manual labor every day of their lives – something he would never be able to fully appreciate.

This moving piece of writing often leads to a discussion of the social marginalization of groups of people in various cultures. The economic exploitation that Rodriguez describes sometimes reminds students of the workers in the second core reading who feel like slaves without any power.

For students choosing Question 1: Rodriguez learned several important things from his summer job. He would never know what "real work" was like as his father had told him (pars. 8–9, 16–17), and he would not be able to lessen the distance between *los pobres* and himself with a little physical labor (par. 16). Additionally, he discovered that there is great diversity among workers and no "single type" (par. 9). Finally, Rodriguez learned that the middle-class American workers he met were not oppressed in the same way as the Mexican laborers who had no "public identity" and were thus extremely vulnerable (pars. 9, 16, 18).

ADDITIONAL READING 3 (pages 278–282)
Action Will Be Taken: An Action-Packed Story Heinrich Böll

In this story about a factory employee, Böll portrays the obsession of his native land, Germany, with organization and efficiency. Unsparing in his use of satire, he criticizes the hypocrisy of Germans who stress the values of action, hard work, and seriousness when, in reality, they can be largely inactive and unproductive.

Students usually enjoy this story, despite its linguistic difficulty, but miss many of Böll's satiric jabs. Before assigning the story, instructors might spend some time discussing the difference between satire (a ridiculing of human weakness) and irony – a type of humor in which an incongruity exists between what is said and what is actually meant, or between the actual result and the expected result. Although satire often employs irony, it doesn't always. Both satire and irony are often hard for students to detect, even for very advanced learners.

Before You Read (page 278)

Before discussing the extent to which the values of action, achievement, and efficiency are stressed in their native culture, refer students to the section "Achievement, Action, Work, and Materialism" (pages 11–12) in the first core reading in Chapter 1, "American Values and Assumptions."

After You Read (page 282)

For students choosing Question 1: The main idea Böll is conveying in the story is the hypocrisy of German society, which stresses the values of action, hard work, and seriousness when, in reality, Germans can remain largely inactive and unproductive. (See the comments about pensiveness and inactivity in pars. 30 and 32.) Böll satirically attacks the German obsession with organization and efficiency, which he sees as a naïve faith similar to the belief in Santa Claus (par. 26).

For students choosing Question 2: Böll uses irony and satire throughout the story to portray the social hypocrisy mentioned in the previous activity. Examples of irony include the question in paragraph 5, the answer in paragraph 10, and Wunsiedel's death as an "action" in paragraph 19. Further examples of irony are the narrator's comment about taking action in paragraph 28; the narrator's new job as a professional mourner in paragraph 32; and the narrator's description of his true vocation at the end of paragraph 32, where inactivity is a "duty." Examples of satire include the narrator's comments in paragraph 11; the activities of the employees in paragraphs 13–15 and 20; and the narrator's repeated statements about action in paragraph 18.

ADDITIONAL READING 4 (page 283)

To Be of Use Marge Piercy

The speaker of this poem describes the things he or she values most in work and people's attitude toward it. People long for useful work that contributes to the good of humanity in some real or evident way. The individuals who should truly be admired are those who, with effort, patience, and enthusiasm, work with others to "do what has to be done, again and again" (line 11). Although the poem, in one sense, is an ode to the common laborer, in another, it is a celebration of any person who "submerges in the task" (lines 12–13) and gets done what has to be done.

Because of Piercy's extensive use of metaphors, most students find this poem, on first reading, quite difficult to understand. After analyzing the figurative language, however, they have a much greater appreciation of Piercy's rather simple message.

After You Read (page 283)

For students choosing Question 1: See the description of the poem, above.

For students choosing Question 2: Words that might be used to describe the major tone of the first three stanzas are *admiration*, *enthusiasm*, and *celebration*. The tones of the final stanza are satisfaction (lines 18–24) and longing (lines 25–26).

ADDITIONAL READING 5 Humor

The Purpose of Work (pages 284–285)

This joke pokes fun at the U.S. values of achievement, action, work, and materialism as described on pages 11–12 of "American Values and Assumptions," the first core reading in Chapter 1. The activities of the South Pacific Islander (par. 6) are similar to those recommended by Walljasper in the third core reading of this chapter. The enjoyment of family, friends, and the small, spontaneous pleasures of life are activities that counter the hectic pace of U.S. life.

Dilbert Cartoon Scott Adams (page 285)

This cartoon pokes fun at the inefficiency and ineptness of company management. Students might be reminded of Böll's satire of German efficiency and organization in the third additional reading.